Author's Note:

This is a fictional account based on two different storms that I've ridden out in my home in Nags Head, NC. Places appearing in the story are fictional, but all based on existing places on the Outer Banks.

I would like to thank my wife Char Smrdel for her unwavering belief in me, even during those periods when I was skeptical in my own abilities.

Thank you also to all my friends that have provided council and enthusiasm to help keep me going during this process. They include: Jennifer Shenberger, Michael Gershe, Kevin Whelan, Bryan Walsh, Joseph LS Terrell and Matt Wolfarth. Without you guys, it is unlikely I would be at this point.

And thank you to you, the reader. I hope you enjoy reading this as much as I enjoyed writing it.

Greg Smrdel

Chapter 1.

It was a beautiful, early evening in fall, picture- perfect. The skies were blue. That shade of blue that the locals would often refer to as "Carolina Blue." The winds were gentle, almost as if they were asking forgiveness as they caressed the cheek of each person they came into contact with. You couldn't ask for a better day. Though many people would take notice of the gorgeous day, few would be able to enjoy it the way it ought to be enjoyed.

Todd Richards, with coffee at his side, was sitting on the roof of his house repairing and replacing shingles. Izzy had done a very good job making sure there was plenty of work to do, not only for Todd, but for all of his neighbors. In this case, Izzy wasn't a spurned ex-girlfriend. No, Izzy was what the weather people had called "The Hurricane of the Century."

Todd was one of the luckier Outer Bankers. His house in Kitty Hawk was 12 feet above sea level, much higher than most on that narrow strip of land. It was about 3/4 of a mile wide and sat between the gray waters of the mighty Atlantic and the mostly calm waters of the sound. If his house was going to be affected by flood waters, then the entire town would be underwater as well. Some were. Virginia Dare Rd, often referred to by locals and tourists alike as "the beach road," was washed away again around milepost 4 1/2 out in front of the Black Pelican restaurant. This 1/4 mile stretch of road had been washed away and rebuilt, due to storms, more often than Kenny Roger's face, despite the fact the sea dune that is supposed to protect it keeps getting built higher and higher each time it is replaced. All of this proving, time and time again, that Mother Nature takes what she wants.

As Todd banged each roofing nail into place, he couldn't help but wonder and pray about whether his best friend in the world, his yellow lab Jack, was safe somewhere on this barrier island. Jack had disappeared before the storm, and now Todd was becoming increasingly worried as each minute, hour, and day passed. In fact, at this point, Todd had the notion that he might never see Jack again.

Jack wasn't just Todd's dog; he was the neighborhood's dog. Sure, Jack would come to Todd's house every day to be fed and find his water, but he didn't exactly "live" there in the strictest sense. The neighborhood kids would often coax Ole Jack off the shade of Todd's deck to come out and play. Together they would all go down to the beach and play in the waves. When the kids went home for dinner, Jack would go back to Todd's deck to eat and bed down for the night in the dog bed that Todd had provided.

Jack was a local hero of sorts, having been written up in the newspaper for saving a couple of those kids from drowning. One time, one of the kids was caught in a rip current and was dangerously being carried further and further out –to- sea. Jack ran to the beach and found a lifeguard patrolling on an ATV. He barked and ran in and out of the water until the guard spotted the swimmer in trouble. Another time, one of the kids exhausted herself out in the water and was able to hold onto Jack's neck while he swam them both safely into the shore. Jack the Hero. That's what the newspaper had called him.

Now Jack was nowhere to be seen. And he hadn't been seen for days….

Chapter 2.

The TV was on the Weather Channel, as it often is when where you live is so affected by wind, rain, and other things that Mother Nature might throw at you. As Todd was up and getting ready for the day, Char, the sexy weather girl, was saying something about a weather disturbance off the coast of Africa. "Nothing yet to be concerned with. But something that we, at the Weather Channel, will be keeping an eye on in the future." Todd, who owns the second largest landscape company on the Outer Banks, made a mental note since he had some large jobs coming up. But he really didn't pay that much attention.

Todd came to the beach almost 30 years ago. A long enough period to have the locals to almost think of him as one of their own, but not quite. Todd was still a "dirty Yankee" to some of the old timers. There were two classifications of people from the north as far as the locals were concerned. There were simple "Yankees." Those were the people that would come down on vacation, spend their money, and then leave. Then there were those who were like Todd--the "dirty Yankees." They were the people from the north who came down and stayed.

Todd lived his childhood and teenage years in Cleveland, Ohio. He moved down to the beach to follow his older brother, Bryant, who came down to become the "Voice of Morning Radio" in Wanchese, at Ocean 105 FM. The Richards family had vacationed on the Outer Banks since the early 70's when there was only one traffic light to be found, the one at Colington Road. Now there seemed to be traffic lights every six feet. It was Bryant who proclaimed that "this is where I'm gonna live one day" on that first family vacation. It seemed that Bryant always wanted to live in some new exotic place, as long as it wasn't Cleveland.

So Bryant got the job, and six months later, Todd moved onto his couch. Ironically, Todd is still on the OBX, and his older brother, Bryant, is back in Cleveland, not even in radio any longer.

At first Todd had a carefree life. He surfed and talked to the pretty vacationing girls on the beach all day. He had dinner prepared each night by Bryant's wife, Jill, and later, he would go out with friends. It was the perfect life for someone who just turned 21, and he enjoyed it for that entire summer. But then two things happened: The season ended, and all the tourists packed up and left. And then Jill decided that enough was enough. For three months, she allowed Todd to live on their couch while she and Bryant worked all day to put food on the table and a roof over their heads. Now it was time for Todd to contribute!

As it turned out, Jill had a friend that had just left his job at the 17-store shopping complex at the beach that she managed. The shopping complex was a destination spot for many of the tourists and locals alike. It had the typical touristy things, but it also had a fur coat and a jewelry store; it always amazed Jill the number of Wanchese fishermen who would come into these stores dressed in bib overalls and bare feet with enough cash to choke a horse. They frequently purchased fur coats or diamond bracelets for their wives. This place truly taught Jill to never judge a book by its cover.

Her friend John, who had been one of the floor salesman, was starting his own landscape business and needed someone to push a lawn mower. As it turned out, Jill had someone on her couch that could do just that! And off Todd went to work with John.

It wasn't that Todd didn't have a work ethic. He did—a strong one. It was just that he lacked discipline in his younger years. He had made it into one of the top rated high schools in the state of Ohio, but he only made it half-way through before transferring to the local public school. It wasn't because he wasn't smart enough; it was because he didn't want to apply himself to what he considered mundane things-- Beowulf, The Canterbury Tales. It made no sense to Todd to have to read and comprehend these unrelatable things.

A few years earlier, right after he moved down to the beach with his brother, Todd was involved in an incident. The local ATM was attacked by a baseball bat when it didn't render him the requested cash. The police made a quick visit to Todd's house as his card was the last one read and the camera had a recording of the transaction, two things Todd hadn't thought about beforehand. Afterwards, Todd had, in the words of Ricky Ricardo (Google it kids), some "splaining" to do! Luckily for Todd, community service was his only punishment for his juvenile crime.

He wasn't a bad kid. He was just a kid that needed some direction, and John and his OBX Landscape Company provided that for him.

So, Todd worked. He pushed the lawnmower. He learned how to dig and install sprinkler systems. He learned landscape design. Soon the OBX Landscape Company grew, largely, but not solely, in part from the sweat from Todd's back. It was only a matter of a few years until Todd owned the company, sans the landscape design department-- John held onto that. Together they had the second largest landscape company in Dare, Hyde, Currituck and Tyrell counties in North Carolina. It was the one most people trusted.

Chapter 3.

Char the weather girl, looking beautiful as always in her official Weather Channel wardrobe, was back on the TV. The disturbance that she promised to keep an eye on had taken greater shape. It had become just a bit more organized as it started drifting west across the Atlantic. Something about it being a tropical wave near the Cape Verde Islands is what Todd thought he heard her say.

Though still not terribly concerned about the weather disturbance, Todd planned out the day for his staff. They had some big jobs coming up, and he wanted to make sure they were ready. He needed to send three guys up north to the Duck-Corolla border to handle the landscape design that John had drawn up for the new Hyatt Hotel being built on the sound front. It wasn't a typical high-rise hotel because of certain town variances, but it would be sprawling and require some attention to detail.

Down south in Rodanthe, yes, that Rodanthe, where Richard Gere and Diane Lane spent nights riding out their own storm in the movie "Nights in Rodanthe," Todd's crew was, ironically, contracted to take care of the famous house from that movie. The new owners wanted new landscaping. They wanted to market the house, as much as was possible, to the next season's tourists. Todd needed to draw up his battle plan for that job and was riding down with his guys that would be doing the work. He would then quickly have to make the close to two-hour drive back up to the job at the Hyatt, all before lunch. Today Jack the dog decided not to play with the neighborhood kids; instead, he accompanied the crew on their endeavors. Somehow, stress levels were always lower when Jack was around. The day was productive and the projects were well underway. The projection for both jobs seemed to point to them being concluded in 10 to 14 days.

It was if the discipline that Todd had lacked all his life suddenly found itself in this business he now co-owned.

Chapter 4.

It's a depression. A tropical depression that is. It had formed near Cape Verde with low level circulation. That is what Char reported on this morning's weather report anyway. A possible intensification might come in the next 24-36 hours. There was nothing to do now but wait and see. It was much too far off to be considered dangerous or even a nuisance, except for the people and property on the East Coast of the United States.

Things were going well for Todd and his crew on both jobs. John had drawn up some new plans for the Hyatt. The owners of the hotel wanted more palm trees, the kind you find in Florida, not the kind you find in North Carolina. Todd thought it was a silly idea, but the tourists always get what they want. "If they want the illusion of swaying palms that are not indigenous to the area, dammit, they will have swaying palms that are not indigenous to the area. Besides, it will mean more money to the bottom line. Thankfully, in this day and age, palms like that are readily available online. Getting them here won't even be a minor inconvenience."
As far as what was going on with the Rodanthe house, that was turning out to be a different story altogether. What few people knew or realized was that the house, after the filming, was condemned. At the time of the movie, the house sat on 400 feet of beach that various storms throughout the years had, not so slowly, washed away. The house was declared a public nuisance and some youths in the area used it as their own personal clubhouse, gaining entry to drink beer and have parties. But recently, the house had been saved, and its owners picked the house up off its piling and trucked it-- that was a day filled with both angst and a little bit of curiosity-- and then moved it to a new location that protected it from Mother Nature's elements.

At the time, the blue shutters that were added for the movie were gone, as were the famous wrap around decks. The new owners wanted to renovate the house back to its original splendor from the movie, both inside and out, and then turn it into a vacation rental. Considerable time and expense had already been put into the project; drawings were made up and supplies had been bought.

All of that was unbeknownst to the OBX Landscape Company at the time of the contract. Todd assumed he and his crew would be able to do their planting and landscape work unencumbered. But from the first day forward, it was evident that they would have to work around the other contractors who were there to do their part of this grand renovation: there were drywallers, carpenters, plumbers, and electricians, along with the city inspectors whose only job seemed to be to make them rip out the previous day's work and start all over again because of minor infraction against the city code. And none of these people gave a damn about stepping on any new flowers or plantings that Todd and his crew, so painstakingly, set into the ground.

One bit of satisfaction came on that first day, however, Jack the dog was there, and so was the dog of one of the interior designers, some little Maltese or some other rat- type dog, who thought he was the alpha animal at the job site. Fifi or Rosie, or some other equally ridiculous name for a dog, decided to get all up in Jack's face. It was quite comical. Jack looked up at Todd, who seemingly approved of what was going through the animal's mind. Todd gave a quick nod, and before anyone noticed what was happening, Jack picked up the little rat dog by the collar and unceremoniously deposited her into the waves of the Atlantic. Score one for the yellow lab!

It reminded Todd of the day that Jack first ran into the Wild Horses of Corolla, but in reverse. Jack merely wanted to play, but ran into a group of four or five horses who didn't want to be bothered. So they kicked poor Jack into the waves as if to say "leave us the hell alone." Fifi or Rosie, or whatever, was certainly not going to cause a ruckus again, although the interior designer certainly did.

Luckily, the Hyatt project was bringing in extra cash with its last-minute addition of the swaying palms, because the project in Roadanthe – where they had to repair all the damage from the other workers-- was turning into a job with very low profit margins. But that's the thing. As a business owner, you would think Todd would care more about that. But in his mind, he already was a winner. He had the sunshine, the beach, his surfing, a group of guys who work for him that he thinks of as family, and he's waking up each morning with his bedroom windows open, listening to the sound of the crashing surf on the ocean. Sure, he could make more money, but that might entail putting on a suit each day and becoming a mindless drone in some huge corporation, and living in Terra Haute, Indiana, or some other such equally depressing northern town. No, for his money, he was quite happy living each of his days in what had come as close to paradise for Todd as any other place on earth. Besides, he still makes a pretty good penny. Sometimes the grass isn't always greener. Or in Todd's case, the sand isn't always finer....

Chapter 5.

Todd wakes up. He listens to the surf for a few minutes through the open bedroom windows and then gets up and goes into the kitchen to turn on the coffee pot. He then steps out onto the deck leading from his bedroom with a large cup filled with strong, black coffee. Out on the deck, Jack is already up and looking for his breakfast. Todd fills the dog's bowl and turns on the Weather Channel to make sure his crew will get in a full day of work. As he sprawls out on the couch on the deck, right on time for her shift, Char, the weather girl, lets him know that all systems are go. The crew will get in their full eight hours and more if they want to stay a little later to get the project ahead of schedule. That's the thing about the OBX Landscape Company; they found the secret to success. Most companies will over promise and under deliver. Todd has figured out that if you just do what you say you're going to do, you're 95% better than most businesses out there. That isn't quite good enough for Todd. His business philosophy has always been to under promise and over deliver! In fact, that is the company's mission statement.

Oh by the way, the tropical depression now has a name--it's Izzy, and she's now a tropical storm.

Chapter 6.

A good day of work is where, at the end of it, you, your crew, and the customer are all equally happy. That is what you strive for, and that's how today has turned out. Todd is so happy with the results that he decided to take all of his guys to The Happy Dolphin for fish tacos. Not just any fish tacos, but the fish tacos that the President once had delivered to the White House via Marine One (just don't tell the taxpayers).

Watching all eight of his guys enjoying the blackened and grilled grouper tacos and the cold Corona's gave Todd a warm glow. He was happy with the life he had created for himself. He started pushing a lawnmower a dozen year ago, and now, he's able to help provide for eight families. Now, if he could only figure a way to stick his partner John with half this bill….

The next day turned out to not be such a good work day. The day brought with it gray and rainy skies. There was wind too, but that is just the usual fare along the Outer Banks. There was too much of a chance of the guys getting hurt, so it was best to just take the day off and catch up on paperwork and returning emails. But who was he kidding? Todd knew that he'd just spend the better part of the day on Netflix watching *The Andy Griffith Show*. After all, Andy once did live, and is now buried just across the sound from him on Roanoke Island. In fact, before dying, Andy was a customer of the OBX Landscape Company. He even did a radio commercial for Todd in exchange for some work on his property.

Chapter 7.

Char was back at her post. Today seemed much better, in terms of the weather. Todd now wondered how Tropical Storm Izzy was coming along way out there in the Atlantic. He didn't have to wait long to find out as the tropical forecast came right up. It now seemed that Izzy had lost some strength and was back down to a tropical depression. "Guess that takes care of that storm," Todd said out loud to no one. When you live along the eastern most part of the Continental United States, you have a tendency to keep an eye towards the east to watch for any potential weather that may be dangerous, or even just a nuisance. That's just how life is along the coast, especially if you own a business where your work is dictated by the weather. Sometimes you work longer; sometimes you work less. It's all up to how Char dictates what Mother Nature will throw at you on any given day. After breakfast and his morning constitution, Jack was in the back yard, something that always got Todd riled up. "He's not my dog. He's the neighborhood dog. Why is it only my yard that he likes to mess up?" As Todd came downstairs to head off to work, Jack jumped into the back of Todd's truck. Apparently, he needed time away from the neighborhood kids today.

Today would be spent at the Rodanthe House. Some of the plants weren't in the ground yet, and Todd was concerned that they may have blown away in yesterday's weather or, more likely, blown away in the back of one of the contractor's trucks. As it turns out, he needn't have worried; the entire inventory was still there. Todd instructed the guys on the layout of each plant and the distance they had to be planted apart from each other so they had room to spread out as they matured. Once everything was explained to the crew, Todd took Jack down to the water's edge.

"It is times like this, it's good to be the boss," he thought to himself. He didn't have to do the grunt work anymore. Hell, he was getting a little too old for that. The one thing that can be said about working landscaping under the hot tropical sun is that your body gets older a little quicker than the average person. Todd and Jack spent a couple hours under the clear, blue Carolina, sunshine-filled skies. Todd watched as Jack went chasing down the beach after some seagulls. It seemed silly that Jack would keep trying like that; he'd never ever caught one, and God knows he'd tried! Both Todd and Jack liked chasing fiddler crabs as they scurried down their burrows built in the sand. They too were much too quick for both man and dog. Jack soon bored of losing to the other animal species on the beach, so he romped over to the piece of driftwood that was bobbing back and forth with each wave. Jack snatched it just as a little rogue wave came and knocked him back several feet onto the shore. Todd knew that he would be spending the next 20 minutes or so doing his best "Nolan Ryan" impression as he threw the driftwood as far as he could so Jack could chase after it and bring it back. Thankfully, it seemed that Jack would tire out at the same point that Todd's arm could no longer take the strain of heaving the piece of wood.

Play time would now be over, and it would be time to check in on the crew and let them break for lunch. As Todd was heading over the protective sand dune back to the work site, he glanced over his shoulder back to the water just in time to see four or five dolphins swim parallel to the shore about 50 yards out. "In search of food," Todd thought. At that moment, the seagulls, being the scavengers that they were, flew out and began trailing the swimming mammals looking for trace pieces of food. "Yes indeed," Todd thought," Life is good in my own slice of paradise."

That feeling of satisfaction was short lived, and once he returned to the job site, Todd discovered that even more of their hard work had been destroyed, this time by the general contractor working on the kitchen rehab. The contractor decided that he would just lay his marble countertops onto something non-abrasive so they wouldn't get scratched or damaged. Apparently, the freshly planted lavender shrubs were the exact right place for this. Todd had gotten back just as one of his guys was about to take a swing at the contractor's head. Fortunately, that encounter was thwarted. But would other fights erupt in the future if he wasn't there? Certainly, Todd thought, he couldn't be on the job site every minute of every day until completion. He could just call off his guys until the inside work was completed. But there were two problems with that: it was in direct opposition to his Mission Statement for the OBX Landscape Company. Remember, they under promise and over deliver on every job! They couldn't afford to take time off from their work. Otherwise, they would never make the job deadline. And secondly, and even more importantly, if his guys didn't work the job, they wouldn't get paid. There was no other job that he could dump them on right now. In most cases, these guys had wives and children to feed. No, a solution had to be found.

Todd rounded up all the contractors --the carpenters, the plumbers, the electricians --and had a quick meeting. He very nicely pointed out to each that his company worked for a lot of wealthy businesses and individuals on the Outer Banks. If each contractor could see their way of being more careful of his crews' work, then when those businesses and individuals asked his opinion about whom to hire for certain jobs, as they often did, he would feel good about recommending them. Each contractor, seeing the logic of what Todd was saying, agreed that they would be more careful.

So, the crisis was averted, and a long 10-hour day was complete. What is it the commercials all say about this time of day? Ah, yes….it's Miller Time! It was time to head to the Happy Dolphin for a quick one, two, or three….

Chapter 8.

It's Saturday. So, there is no work today, not for Todd or his crew. As is his habit, the Weather Channel is on and a coffee is in his hand. It must not be a work day for Char either as some hairy guy named Bob, dressed in a suit that seems about two sizes too small, is on the TV. It's not as pleasing to watch today.

Nothing was mentioned about Izzy. "Must be another storm that just went away," Todd thought.

It was going to be a pretty day on the Outer Banks with temperatures in the 80's and calm winds. It wasn't going to be a surf day, but it would be a great day to head over to Roanoke Island and do some stand- up paddle boarding with Chuck.

Chuck and Todd had been friends for years. Their friendship lasted longer than the relationship that Todd had with Chuck's sister, Kim. Todd and Kim dated off and on for about three years. She was a stereotypical surfer girl with blonde, flowing hair, who didn't need or use much makeup. A real "earthy chick" Is how Todd described her. Kim was a free spirit and never really got why Todd was so devoted to his work. She was more of the mindset that if the waves were pumping anywhere between the northern beaches and Hatteras, you went surfing. On her priority list, earning a living was way below surfing. In fact, everything to Kim was less important than surfing. Chuck was a bit more balanced than his sister. He also was always on the water--paddle boarding, surfing, kite surfing, wind surfing, kayaking--but he was able to combine his passions into his work life.

Chuck was the owner and operator of the Roanoke Island Outfitters Group, a company that rented out water sports equipment and provided guide services for various kayaking expeditions across the "Tar Heel State." They had even ventured into South Carolina and Virginia.

Todd and Kim had remained civil and even friendly since deciding to go their separate ways. There would always be a spark between them, an ember that would never fade, but it was too much of opposites attract, apparently. The best thing to come out of that relationship was the friendship Todd and Chuck had formed- a bromance, Kim would always kiddingly say, despite the fact that Chuck had been happily married to his 8th grade sweetheart from Manteo Middle School.

A quick cup of coffee, some scrambled eggs, and a sweet potato biscuit made by Chuck's wife, Trish, and Todd and Chuck were out the door. If he could, Todd would have come over seven days a week, 52 weeks a year for Trish's sweet potato biscuit. That was worth the 30-minute drive alone. After breakfast, Todd and Chuck decided to head to downtown Manteo, just a short walk down the street, to put their paddle boards in the water at the public boat ramp near the bridge to Ice Plant Island and Festival Park.

The water was as smooth as glass, nary a ripple, and the paddling was easy. They headed out the canal and into the open water of the sound. With the calm conditions, no sailboats would be out today creating an obstacle- free day on the water. Off at about their 3 o'clock, as they hit open water, was some sort of marine life. It could be bull shark, which were often swimming in the warm, brackish, shallow waters of the sound. Most people didn't realize it, but they were usually there.

Recently, there was even a report of a bull shark as far upriver on the Mississippi as Illinois. More than likely though the marine life would turn out to be dolphins. There was a group of four kayakers who rented their boats from Chuck that were in hot pursuit of them, whatever they were. That was part of the beauty and charm of living in such a place; you could interact with the dolphins in their own environment.

Because Chuck's business was also weather dependent, Todd knew that Chuck would be keeping an eye on the weather disturbance off the Cape Verde Islands. Chuck also saw that Tropical Storm Izzy had been downgraded back to a depression. He knew that sometimes that happens and then redevelops back into a powerful storm. But that didn't seem to be what Izzy was likely to do. Todd and Chuck both agreed that that was the last they would see or hear of Izzy.

There is nothing like a beautiful day on the water to help rejuvenate one's soul. Today was exactly what Todd needed after a long week of working with the Hyatt people and the contractors at the Rodanthe House. Just as they made their way back down the canal and to dry land, Trish texted to say that she and Kim were at Pete's on the Water (more often referred to as PW's), and to come meet them for a bucket of clams and a pitcher of beer. Never one to pass up an offer of clams and beer, the boys walked the block down the docks to PW's.

Sometimes Todd found it difficult to hang with Kim in a social setting, especially when her natural free-spirit would cause her to flirt with the fishermen and tourists that would hang out at PW's. Tonight, she was on her best behavior, and the night went by without incident.

Chapter 9.

Todd woke up with the early light and immediately felt remorse for waking up in Kim's bed. He didn't want to fall into that pattern again. It was a pattern that never seemed to work out to his advantage. He was always the one who was getting hurt; Kim always came out the other end of each break-up completely unscathed. If this continued, he knew that would be the case again.

Thankfully, the night before, Kim had heard about a possible swell coming in at the point on Cape Hatteras, so she was up and gone in her Jeep, chasing the surf before Todd got up. She loved that Jeep. It was black, always had the doors off, and the top down. She would throw her boards in the back, along with a backpack full of snacks and a thermos of coffee, and down the beach she would ride. At least with her gone, there would be no awkward conversations; he could just get into his truck and head back over to his house in Kitty Hawk. So, Todd got up, went to the outside shower, got cleaned up, dressed, and left.

Todd didn't head straight home. First there was a stop to grab another sweet potato biscuit. I mean, why not? He was just down the street. As Todd entered Chuck and Trish's house, he was met by a mixed set of reactions--a frown from Chuck and a smile from Trish. If Todd was in their kitchen this morning, they knew where he spent the night, and it wasn't at home in Kitty Hawk.

Todd had the whole day in front of him, free from any obligations. As he left the island and drove across the Manteo-Nags Head Causeway back to the beach, he remembered that his beloved Cleveland Indians were deadlocked in a 1-1 weekend series tie against those hated New York Yankees.

The Happy Dolphin had the MLB package, and Todd knew he could watch the game there. But first he stopped at home for a change of clothes.

Todd pulled into the driveway and was met by Jack who gave him this look as if to say, "Dude, seriously? I know where you've been. Now, how about some food?" Both he and Jack went out onto the deck. Jack ate while Todd sat with his coffee. After they finished, Todd took Jack (or was it the other way around?) over to the sound. They walked out onto the pier to play their favorite game. Todd would throw a tennis ball out into the water as far as he could while Jack would jump off the end of the pier, swim to the ball, swim back to the shore, and then run down the length of the pier and drop the ball. Then he'd be ready to do it all again.

Jack, after all, was a yellow Labrador retriever, and that's what they did. The tourists always loved watching this game of throw, swim, retrieve, and repeat. In fact, Todd had caught the attention of a few of the tourist girls with this game. "Best way to meet women," he always said.

It was now closing in at around 1pm. The game would be starting shortly. Todd and Jack walked the short distance back home. All the way, Jack shaking the wetness out of his fur while Todd got splattered. When they got home, Jack laid down under the house in the shade and fell asleep. Apparently, he was up guarding the empty house all night. Todd grabbed his wallet and keys and headed out for the Happy Dolphin.

On the short drive over, Todd recalled his days as a kid going to watch the Indians with his big brother, Bryant, at the old Cleveland Municipal Lakefront Stadium. That place was cavernous. When 25,000 baseball fans would sit in there on a sunny afternoon, it still felt empty. Most of the 73,000 seats would be vacant. Todd and Bryant loved it. It seemed they always got an entire row to themselves, and they knew the hot dog guy by name. "As a matter of fact, whatever happened to Ol' Jim the hot dog guy?" Todd wondered. The Indians were now in a new(ish) ballpark. When it first opened, it was named Jacobs Field after its owner Dick Jacobs. However, it was more commonly referred to as "The Jake." But now with all the corporate naming of things for millions of dollars a year (like pro sports needed more money), it was called Progressive Field. It was named for a very large insurance company whose headquarters were in town. To Todd, and seemingly thousands of others, the stadium had been and always would be quite simply known as "The Jake."

As Todd pulled into the Happy Dolphin, he already noticed the cars of other local Cleveland Indian fans. This is where they created their own "Tribe Backers Club." No matter where you went in the country, you could always find pockets of Cleveland Indians, Cleveland Browns, and Ohio State Buckeye fans, and the Outer Banks was no different. The National Anthem was playing as Todd took his seat at the far end of the bar that, legend has it, was made out of the timbers of an old 1895 shipwreck that occurred right outside the front door. There was no reason to doubt the legend. After all, this is the stretch of water known as the "Graveyard of the Atlantic." There were more shipwrecks off these waters, per square mile, than any other place in the world. During these times, the locals largely made their living as land pirates.

They would retrieve whatever would wash ashore and either repurpose it, or-- more likely-- sell it. Finders keepers was the law here back then. Modern technology, such as radar, have made the area a bit more safe for shipping, but still, the ever changing shoals made it interesting for boat captains at times.

"It must have been an exciting time to live," Todd often thought. There was something romantic about making your living as a pirate, even if it was a land pirate.

Two Red Stripe beers, three blackened grouper tacos, and an Indians' victory later, Todd squinted as he walked back out into the late afternoon sun. As was his custom during the Indians' games, Todd left his cell phone in the car, wanting to be able to enjoy every pitch without interruption. There were three missed calls and two texts from Kim. That was not what he wanted to see at the moment; he really didn't want to open that can of worms again. His life had been going great lately, free from drama, and he had no interest in returning to a complicated relationship. Spending the night last night was stupid, stupid, stupid. He should have just gone home, or at the very least, sacked out on Chuck and Trish's couch. But it was too late for that, the damage had been done, and he knew sooner or later he would have to deal with it, but not now. Now it was time for a late afternoon nap. (That's what two beers in the afternoon will do to you.) Twenty minutes later, Todd was sound asleep in his hammock on the deck with Jack lying off to his side in his own bed.

As the skies were starting to darken and the sun fell behind the horizon to the west over the sound and Roanoke Island, Todd woke up from his nap.

Earlier in the day, before heading out to the Happy Dolphin, Todd had taken some tuna out of the freezer that he and Chuck caught while out deep sea fishing about a month ago. There was a good-sized tuna steak for himself and a smaller one for Jack. Todd threw them on the grill and cooked them to a perfect medium-rare temperature. He often thought if the landscape business ever went belly up, he could be a cook at a seafood house, or he could make someone a great house husband with his culinary skills. He and Jack devoured their tuna steaks in a matter of minutes.

Todd then reckoned he better hit this Kim thing head- on, so he decided to call her. Thankfully, to his cowardly heart, he got her voicemail. "Hi, this is Kim. If you know me, and you know there are waves, you know why I didn't answer. Leave your message at the beep. And if there's a break in the surf, I'll call you back." Beeeeeep. Todd just simply said that he got her messages and was calling back.

Todd's thoughts then turned to his work tomorrow. Both projects were going to command a lot of his time and energy, so Todd decided to clear his head to prepare for the upcoming stress. He started to walk down to the beach where his intention was to just spend an enjoyable evening alone, just him and his thoughts. About a half a block into his walk, he was overtaken by Jack, who also wanted to go along. The two best friends, neither one owning the other, walked happily down to the water's edge and just sat. That's it. They just sat and watched each wave as it crashed onto shore, while Todd wondered where each wave first started: Was it off the coast of Africa? Did each wave make it all the way across the Atlantic? Was each wave once part of the Tropical Storm Izzy?

Chapter 10.

Todd rarely needed an alarm to wake- up on a work day. His internal clock, for whatever reason, automatically woke him at 6:30 each morning. Researchers say that it's better to naturally wake-up each morning than it is to be startled awake by a loud noise or loud music.

Once out of bed, Todd went through the same daily routine--get up, turn on the coffee pot, head downstairs to the outside shower, head back upstairs, pour a cup of the now ready coffee, grab a piece of toast with peanut butter, head-out to the deck to feed Jack, and turn on the Weather Channel. And just like clockwork, there she was. Char is back at her post with the tropical update as Todd wondered for a quick moment why Kim couldn't be as dependable.

There was probably nothing to see since it was unlikely another disturbance would start brewing so soon after Izzy blew herself out, but he was wrong. Chuck said that sometimes this happens, but neither thought it would. It seems that at some point over the weekend, Izzy had gathered enough strength and re-intensified into a tropical storm again. Tropical Storm Izzy was once again something worth keeping an eye on. During the last couple of days, the storm generally moved westward, due to a strong region of high atmospheric pressure. "Nothing more to be done at this point other than to keep a watch on her," stated Char.

Today is Monday. It was the start of a new week, and the palms were expected to be delivered today to the Hyatt project. Todd was just going to have to place his faith in the fact that everything was ironed out on Friday with his guys and the contractors down in Rodanthe and that no new blowouts were going to occur. They couldn't; he was tied to the northern beaches today at this project.

Jack decided to be lazy today and not come to work, the life of a dog. It was just as well. Todd knew that today was going to be a hectic one with more than two dozen palm trees to deal with. Todd and the crew had both front-end loaders on site. Two of the guys trailered them up from the shop. They were going to need them both to dig the holes and to move the trees around to their new resting place, shading the new pool in the courtyard and around the porte –coche'res.

The delivery truck with the trees made the approximately 75-mile drive down from Norfolk to the Hyatt arriving at 9 a.m., just in time to begin a full day of getting them into place. It was a full day that they put in too. The temperature hung in the mid 80's. Thank goodness for the constant ocean breeze; it made the day's work a bit more bearable.

It was about 7 p.m. when the last tree was finished. It ended up being an 11-hour day, and it was only Monday. Todd already was thinking that at some point during the week he was going to have to give his guys a break. It was time to clean things up, load the front loaders back on their trailers, and drive them back to the shop. On the way back, Todd stopped at the Food Lion in Kitty Hawk to buy the guys a case of beer, a half dozen steaks, and a bag of charcoal. He had the grill going before they got back. They all sat there and enjoyed their meal and beer before heading out into the darkness and off to a good night's sleep, something they certainly earned.

Todd bought and made an extra steak on purpose; he knew that after a long day like this, he was going to be coming home to a very hungry, and therefore, very surly dog. But all was forgiven when Jack made short work of the T-bone.

Chapter 11.

It was a new day and time for a new tropical update. According to Char, the Air Force reserve 53rd Weather Reconnaissance Squadron, commonly referred to as "The Hurricane Hunters" based at Keesler Air Force base in Biloxi, Mississippi, were readying themselves to fly into Izzy to gather more information.

They were an interesting bunch. They fly their Lockheed WC-130J's directly into a hurricane, typically penetrating the eye several times per mission at altitudes of somewhere between 500 and 10,000 feet. From there, they gather weather data that is sent back to the National Hurricane Center to aid them to more accurately forecast, not only the intensity of the storm, but its movement as well. "That means," Todd thought, "if they're mobilizing these guys to potentially fly into the storm, it is likely to turn into a full fledged hurricane fairly soon." But for now, it was still a tropical storm and work was waiting for the OBX Landscape Company at both ends of the beach.

After spending the day up north with the Hyatt project yesterday, Todd was happy to find no new flare-ups occurred down south at the Rodanthe House. A fair amount of work had been completed in his absence yesterday, but a fair amount still needed to be done. Now the owners wanted to include some plants and flowers in pots scattered about the decks that were once again going to be built to match the appearance of the house from the movie, which meant jumping onto the online webpage of the nursery he used most often in Tidewater, Virginia. He'd need to order both the plants and the pots to put them in. He wished that he had known ahead of time that this was how he was going to spend his day; he could have stayed home to do it on the comfort of his own deck with Jack lazily lounging next to him.

Jack had no inclination to jump into the truck this morning for the drive to the job site. It was almost like he knew that he'd be wasting his day. Todd sometimes wondered who was smarter-- the guy with the imagination and the opposable thumbs, or the furry animal that takes life as it comes and decides that day what he'd like to do with his time?

The day passed without incident. The ordered materials would be ready tomorrow. To save on the delivery cost, Todd would drive up to Virginia tomorrow to get them all himself. He'd already lost some money on the profit end with some damaged plants. Besides, his guys could get along without him for a half-a-day, not to mention, that a nice, four hour-round trip- road trip was sometimes just what he needed to clear his head.

On his way back home at the end of the day, Todd was thinking it was strange that Kim never tried to reach back out again. Of course, right at that moment when he was feeling good about that, the phone rang; it was Kim. He let it ring three or four times while deciding whether or not to pick it up. She expected that he wouldn't. Todd wasn't good at meeting relationship confrontation head- on. But before it switched over to voicemail, he answered with, "I know. I know. You're surprised that I answered."

Startled by that response, she came back with, "Yeah. Guess I kinda am."

She then followed up with, "No worries. There's no pressure from me about Saturday night. I just wanted to let you know that it was a great night and all, but that's where it started and ends. I love the fact that we've remained friends, and I think that's where we should be right now-- nothing more, nothing less."

Now it was Todd's turn to be startled. "Gee, that's great Kim. I also feel like we are where we're supposed to be. I'm just not at a point where I can give more than I have."

Kim replied, "Great. Well, have a great night. Maybe we can do something this weekend...as friends. Love you."

"Sure. Love you too."

"Wait! What just happened here?" Todd wondered if he had just been bamboozled. He pondered that the rest of the drive home.

When Todd got home, Jack was nowhere to be seen. No doubt he was out with the neighbor kids somewhere. Todd knew as soon as he cranked up the grill to throw some grouper on the embers of the charcoal that Jack would be back soon enough.

One grouper, a baked potato, some asparagus, and two Red Stripe beers later, Todd decided to turn on the TV to see if anything more had become of Tropical Storm Izzy. According to Hairy Bob, the weather guy that filled in for Char over the weekend, the Hurricane Hunters would be leaving Keesler Air Force Base at first light.

"That is not a good sign," Todd thought, as he flipped over to one of his favorite shows, "Wicked Tuna - OBX." Todd knew some of the fishermen on the show, and he always loved watching them kick the New Englanders' asses at their own game. Tonight's episode featured a father and son fishing team from Wanchese. Todd knew the dad pretty well as they had become friends over the years.

Chapter 12.

Todd had fallen asleep with the TV on. Jack was back on the deck outside the French doors that lead to the bedroom. The grouper, that Todd had left out, was gone. It was tough to know if it was Jack or a local raccoon that had gotten to it first. Todd got up and got cleaned up. He poured a large cup of coffee and fed Jack while waiting for the latest tropical storm update.

"It sure is better looking at Char than it was Hairy Bob first thing in the morning," he thought. It turns out that the Hurricane Hunters had gone out and had already recorded winds in the storm at 78 MPH at a height of 1,500 feet, that's four miles per hour higher than the 74 MPH needed for a storm to be considered a hurricane. On the Safire-Simpson wind scale, Izzy was now considered a Category 1 hurricane. That's exactly what the National Hurricane Center called her on this Wednesday morning. Her position was 465 miles east-northeast of the Lesser Antilles, the islands that form the eastern boundary of the Caribbean Sea with the Atlantic Ocean.

While Izzy is now a hurricane, she's still too far off to be of any consequence to the Outer Banks. There are at least a half dozen ways she can go without affecting the barrier islands of North Carolina.

Todd climbed into his truck. Jack wanted to go along today, but since Todd had to drive to South Eastern Virginia and back, he didn't think it was a good idea. Besides, Jack was probably just feeling guilty for being out all night, if animals can feel such things.

In the truck, Todd tuned to Ocean 105. It had been a while since Todd listened to the station, not since his older brother, Bryant, and his wife, Jill, packed up and moved onto a bigger and better radio station in Ohio years ago. So why was he listening now? He didn't know. Perhaps he was feeling a little nostalgic.

As the day broke into sunlight, Todd turned the truck north towards the bridge over to Currituck County and ultimately to Norfolk. It was a cool morning, perfect for a trip up north to get his materials. It was just him, the sun, the breeze, and his thoughts. There was plenty of time to reflect on yesterday's phone conversation with Kim. In fact, it was too much damn time.

After a quick stop at Hardee's for an egg biscuit and large coffee before getting to the North Carolina - Virginia border, Todd made it to the nursery just as it opened for the day. He got all the plants and other materials loaded into the truck and made the return trip back to the Outer Banks, all the way down to the Rodanthe House.

Todd always enjoyed these trips to pick things up. Typically, it allowed him to sort things out in his mind. He liked the peace. He liked the solitude. It was when he would do a lot of planning and decision making. Today was different. He kept dwelling on yesterday's phone call with Kim. Something uneasy was stirring inside, and he couldn't put his finger on it. He just felt like this black cloud was now lying heavy on his shoulders and it was going to erupt into a huge storm.

This uneasiness must have been outwardly evident too. His crew, much like the family that they are, knew something was wrong, something was inwardly disturbing Todd. Because when Todd returned to the job site that day, he was a bit snappy and not his normal, cheery self.

Instead, he kept reminding them all of the impending deadline, and he rushed the guys into unloading the truck and getting everything laid out. They had to get everything planted into the pots and placed along the deck before day's end, along with the other dozen or so things that still had to be done.

The day dragged. The kind of dragging that Todd imagined most people experience when they're sitting in their cubicles figuratively chained to their desks, their only source of light coming from the overhead fluorescent bulbs. The thought of that made him shudder. But in a way, it kicked him in the ass and back to reality. He was always opposed to a life of being a sheep, and he reminded himself just how lucky he was living on the beach and being outside every day in the sunshine. It really makes life's trials and tribulations seem less stressful. Thinking about all of that, almost made him smile.

The end of the day came. The day's checklist was completed, and it was time to head home to Kitty Hawk after a long day. He knew Jack would be waiting for him today since he wasn't able to come along. Along the way, Todd contemplated calling Kim. He was trying to feel out "the lay of the land," what was going on in her head. Sure they had said "I love you" to each other before, but this time, it seemed so easy and natural. Being a coward about these things, he couldn't bring himself to call her. He wasn't in the proper frame of mind for what could be a rather lengthy, drawn out conversation.

Physically and mentally tired from the day, Todd didn't even prepare dinner for himself. The two bottles of Red Stripe would have to serve that purpose tonight. As he lay in bed, his eyes getting heavy, he started drifting off to sleep, and an old rhyme came to mind -- "Red skies at night"...zzzzzzzzzzzzzzzzz.

Chapter 13.

Up and at 'em, Todd was back up without the alarm at 630; it was time to jump into his regular routine. He turned on the coffee pot, headed downstairs to the outside shower to wash the sleep off his body, poured the coffee, fed Jack, and turned on the weather report.

Just like clockwork, there was Char with the local forecast for another glorious day for the Outer Banks. But Todd already knew that-- "Red skies at night," remember? No, he was more interested in the tropical update.

Since moving in a generally westerly direction, Izzy was now turned more to the north-northwest, after two other weather disturbances weakened the ridge that was initially pushing Izzy to the west. Izzy was still well offshore, and it was too early to tell if she would amount to anything. In his bones, Todd was a bit uneasy about it. Then again, it seems he'd been feeling uneasy about a lot of things lately.
Today was Thursday. There were only a couple more days until the weekend, and only one more until TGIF. TGIF always confused Todd, "Thank God it's Friday?"
"Why is most of the world thanking God it's Friday?" Todd wondered. "Friday is still a work day, right? Shouldn't it be TGIS-- Thank God it's Saturday? Or at the very least TGIFAFPM -- Thank God It's Friday After Five PM! "

Todd had a breakfast date today with Chuck. Although Todd tried his best to get Chuck to bring one of Trish's sweet potato biscuits with him, they decided to meet at Harpers at the Outer Banks Mall instead. Harpers is a breakfast and lunch place that seemingly only the locals have discovered. Besides, they have the best crab omelets in the entire county; they just didn't have the best sweet potato biscuit, but second best would have to do.

It was rare that Chuck would be able to get away like this during the day, especially on a day as nice as this as there would be plenty of locals and tourist alike that would want to rent stand-up boards and kayaks. But Chuck was confident his staff would be able to handle the morning's business. In fact, he'd been trying to pull away from doing the day-to-day business lately; he'd worked hard for years and now wanted to enjoy some of the fruits of that labor.

"See the latest tropical storm update report?" Todd asked.

Chuck, knowing that Todd was a freak about such things, made sure he tuned in this morning to address what he knew would be the first subject matter of the day. "Yup," he answered. "I see Ol' Izzy swirlin' out there. But she's small, barely even a hurrikin' at 78 MPH. And waaaaaay too far off to know if she's gonna be a problem or not. In fact, they're not even really paying attention to her on the local radio stations. Outside of me and you, I'm guessing no one here even knows Izzy even exists. Here, I'll prove it to you." When Becky the server came back to refill their coffee cups, Chuck took the opportunity to prove his point.

"Hey Beck, hear about Izzy?"

Becky, always with her ear to the ground on the local gossip looked surprised and said. "No, she a friend of you and Trish?"

"See? My point exactly! "Todd, you gotta stop worrying about these storms all the time."

Todd figured Chuck was right. They finished up their crab omelets and coffee, and the subject of Kim never came to the surface; Todd figured one storm at a time was enough.

It was another busy day ahead, so Todd bid his friend a good day and off to work he went. Todd wanted to visit both work sites today and figured that since he was already at milepost 15, he would head south to Rodanthe first. He would circle back up north to the Duck-Corolla line before heading home for the day.

Todd got to Rodanthe at about 10 a.m., just in time to find no one on his crew working. In fact, no one was--not the carpenters, not the electricians, not the plumbers. It seemed the town had put a halt on everything due to the owners of the house not pulling all the right permits. Apparently, when you move a house from one location to another, there's more than just the usual amount of permits and paperwork needed. Todd knew all the town's officials from one end of the beach to the other and pleaded down at city hall that his work shouldn't be dictated by permits; he was a landscaper, after all, and he wasn't making any structural changes of any sort. Todd's arguments fell onto deaf ears. There were some concerns about whether the house would be allowed to stay where it was and that any work on it would be futile in the event that it would have to be moved again. Knowing when he had hit a brick wall, Todd decided to pull up all stakes on the job. At last word, it was unlikely any more work would be done there for the remainder of the week. This meant that the time table for the job's completion was now in a state of limbo. Wanting to get his guys a full day's work, and with it, a full day's pay, Todd took his guys and made the nearly one-hour drive to The Hyatt work site. "Might as well double-up the workforce there and get things done quicker," he thought. If it got done early, he could always bring both teams down to Rodanthe on a final push to get that job completed. Todd knew a certain amount of choreography was going to have to be put into place so they wouldn't be tripping over each other the remainder of the week.

To make the best use of the work force, he put the Rodanthe crew inside to get the interior landscape design going. There was going to be a large atrium area where the outdoor pool would be turned into an indoor pool during inclement weather. The roof would be retractable, much like some of the modern baseball and football stadiums around the country. The only major difference is that the walls would also be retractable to either fully enclose the pool or to make it totally an outside space. Todd didn't understand the mechanics or the science of how it worked, but damn, it was cool as hell!

So, the Rodanthe crew started mapping out where each plant bed and rock garden was to be located. They had sand trucked in and set into places where it was needed. It always amazed Todd that he had to pay to have sand trucked in when he had a seemingly endless supply of it right outside the front door, but such were the ways of business. Outside, the regular Hyatt crew, happy to see that they had help for at least a couple of days, continued to lay out sections of sod in the courtyard and lay the sprinkler system that would keep that grass lush and green during the hot, dry days of summer. While helping the sprinkler crew with their manual labor, Todd glanced out- at- sea and wondered what storms might be brewing— storms, plural. There was Hurricane Izzy and, quite possibly, Hurricane Kim to contend with in the ensuing days ahead. Both of them had the potential of leaving a wide path of destruction behind them.

Chapter 14.

There it was. Even Char was saying it now, "TGIF." It was just one of those minute things that stuck in Todd's craw. As of the latest tropical update, Hurricane Izzy was now passing about 150 miles north of Anegada, the only inhabited British Island formed by coral and limestone rather than being born from volcanic activity. It was also the northern most island in the Lesser Antilles. Izzy was still churning as a minimal Category 1 hurricane prompting hurricane warnings for the area. "As it inches closer to this side of the Atlantic, more people will start taking notice," Todd thought.

Both crews reported for duty on this Friday at the Hyatt job site. Todd made a quick phone call to a friend in the offices of the town where the Rodanthe House was located and quickly found out the house was still tied up in red tape. Although, all concerned promised to do their best to get it all sorted out today. This meant no work by anyone today on the house. But Todd could at least now throw double the work force at the Hyatt job.

While the crew made themselves busy on the day's duties-- one set of guys inside, one outside-- Todd decided to walk down to the beach and do something uncharacteristic; he decided to call Kim. He had no idea if she went to work today or if she got an early surf report from one of her friends down south and ran down there instead, but he decided to give it a try. Todd thought Kim was lucky that her brother Chuck was also her employer, not many others would be so understanding when it came to her work ethic.

"Hello?"

"Hey Kim. What's up?"

"Todd?"

"Yeah, who else? Never mind. Strike that question."

"Funny. It's just that I didn't think you knew cellphones also allowed you to call out. You so rarely call. Come to think of it, you hardly ever answer either."

Todd, blushing slightly, knew she was right. He wasn't one for phones, except for business use. He wasn't much of a chit-chatter. "Yeah, I know. Just had a break in the action and decided I'd just see how you're doing."

"Um, ok. I'm, uh, fine. You?"

"Yeah, good. Didn't know if you were working or surfing today, but decided to give it a try."

"Well, believe it or not, Kallie did call and wanted to go surfing. But, I don't know. I decided to come in and help Chuck out today. He's been trying to move away from the day- to-day, and I just thought maybe his little sister should help him a bit more."

Todd was taken aback by that answer. Kallie was Kim's best surf buddy, and when Kallie called, Kim typically dropped everything and ran out to the waves. "Wow!" Todd replied, "Is little Kim starting to get responsible?"

"Shut up you ass! Just because my priorities are a bit different from yours doesn't make me irresponsible. My mortgage gets paid. My utilities get paid, as do all my other financial obligations. Just because I have little left over and because I choose to have some fun in this life, doesn't make me irresponsible."

"Whoa, you're right. Settle down. I didn't mean to open that can of worms. And truth be told, I wish I had a little more of you in me. Sometimes it's tiring being the guy who has to hold everything together all the time! Well, since you're working, I'll let you go. You have any plans tonight?"

"Well, I could work some overtime tonight…."

With that, they both broke out laughing.

"No, of course not silly. What did you have in mind?"

"I don't know. Nothing formal. How about coming over to the house, and I'll make us dinner. Jack hasn't seen you in forever, and I know he'd love for you to throw him the tennis ball from the pier."

"Yeah, that sounds nice. How about 7?"

"Perfect. Been a while. Remember how to get there?"

"Jackass. Yes, I remember how to get there." And with that, she hung up the phone.

At that moment, Todd had a few emotions running through him. He felt happy, scared, and confused. "What the hell did I just do?" He screamed at the ocean.

Todd wrapped up the workday a little early. He figured that they had gotten more work done than anticipated at the Hyatt project, so why not let the guys enjoy their weekend a bit early? Oh, who was he kidding? He knocked off early because he painted himself into a corner with Kim, and now he had to run around before 7. He had to run to Food Lion since the refrigerator was bare, and he had to clean up the house.

For a guy, Todd pretty much had a clean house. The hardwood floors could use a mopping, and every guy's bathroom can use some sort of cleaning, at least for it to be up to a woman's standards.

As Todd was putting the finishing touches on the low country boil that he decided to make for dinner, he heard the wheels of Kim's jeep crunch on the gravel driveway below the house. For some reason, butterflies had picked this moment to erupt in his stomach. He'd never been nervous before with Kim, so why now?

Kim came bounding up the steps to the house. Wearing a white sundress that fully accentuated her tan, she was carrying a bottle of Todd's favorite Pinot Noir. Todd was typically a beer guy, but occasionally, he liked to indulge in a nice glass of red wine.

"Hi. Smells wonderful in here," Kim said as she came through the door.

"Yeah, thanks. I remembered how you like my low country boil. Here, let me open the bottle and get us a glass of wine while the crabs finish up."

"Why Todd, I do declare! You are such the gentleman tonight. Almost like a dirty Yankee is trying to woo this little ol' southern girl."

Slightly embarrassed and full on blushing, Todd opened the bottle, poured two glasses, and finished preparing the dinner.

They sat down and had a nice dinner on the deck. The shade from the massive trees provided a comfortable place to eat outside.

Jack sat beneath the table and was eating the pieces of crab that Kim would sneak to him when Todd wasn't looking. Todd was always one for wanting to be outside and not cooped up inside. For that matter, Kim was the same. Todd talked about his two ongoing work projects. Kim talked about her wanting to help Chuck out some more at the store. The two grownups finally had a grown- up conversation.

"There's still about an hour of daylight left. You up for going out on the pier and throwing Jack the ball and letting him work off some of that crab you fed him?"

Kim, knowing that she had been caught, giggled softly and nodded yes.

Todd, Kim, and Jack walked out to the sound with the tennis ball. "This time, try not to throw like a girl," Kim said to Todd, knowing that once upon a time, in a different life, Todd had been an all-city third baseman.

"Don't you worry. I'll try not to embarrass you."

"You sure you want me standing next to you?" Kim said. "Won't it hurt your chances of you and Jack picking up some tourist girl?"

This time it was Todd's turn to call Kim an ass.

The sun slipped under the horizon and day started turning into night. It was like that sign says that hangs above the pool at Chuck's house: "The sun loved the moon so much that he died every night so she may live." With that, they walked back to the house arm in arm.

Chapter 15.

It was Saturday morning. The sun was up. Todd was up, and so were Jack and Hairy Bob with the Tropical forecast. Kim was still sleeping, so Todd let her be and went to watch the TV in the living room, the one he never uses; he didn't want to disturb sleeping beauty.

It appears that while Todd and Kim were having a good time, so was Hurricane Izzy. She had strengthened into a major hurricane, which put her at a Category 3 hurricane, at the very least. This occurred while passing northeast of the Bahamas. At some point since the last update, Izzy had quickly intensified and developed an eye that stretched ten miles wide, surrounded by an eye wall. The eye wall is the ring of thunderstorms where the most severe weather occurs. The Hurricane Hunters were being called upon to fly another mission into her to extrapolate the latest information on her strength and movement. Todd was more than a little concerned at this point.

Kim was soon awake, and the two decided to grab some breakfast at Harper's. This was the second night they'd spent together out of the last seven. That hadn't happened in nearly six months, and Todd wasn't sure what to make of it all. But he was surprised he wasn't feeling like he needed to run away.

They went to Harper's because it was in the direction of Roanoke Island, and Kim had promised Chuck that she'd help out in the store by 10 am. Besides, Todd also wanted to go into the store. He had been thinking about buying another stand-up board, and if Kim got the commission on it, well, that wouldn't be a bad thing.

After Todd finished his sausage gravy and biscuit and Kim her bowl of fresh fruit, they grabbed a coffee to go, and then each one headed to the Roanoke Island Outfitters in their own vehicles; Todd wanted to talk to Chuck about the latest tropical update.

"Top O' the morning to you Sis," Chuck cheerfully greeted Kim as she came through the door. "Should be a busy day today. Thanks for coming in."

"No worries Big Bro. Always glad to help." They both started laughing hysterically because they both knew she would rather be shredding waves at the point.

About a minute and a half later, Todd, trying to be nonchalant, walked in. "Oh geez. Must be more ominous storm updates this morning for you to be here," Chuck said upon seeing his friend.

"You didn't see the report this morning dude?" Todd asked.

"No, but if you're here, I'm guessing there's something I should know."

Todd gave Chuck a quick update about Izzy strengthening into a major hurricane and the forming of a well-defined eye wall. Chuck thought that perhaps he should also pay attention to the latest updates, just in case.

Todd walked over to Kim. "Well, Miss. I might be in the market for a new paddle board. Got anything you can show me?"

"Well, Sir. Um. What's your name again?" She asked coyly.

"Uh, Todd. But you can call me Mr. Richards."

"Well, Mr. Richards. You seem like a big spender. And, oh, is that a Yankee accent I detect? How about one of these top of the line Surftech Sabers? I think I can let it go for about $1,200.00."

Todd gulped. "That does come with the 40% friends and family discount, yes?"

Chuck intervened. "Come on Kim. Quit picking on the Yankee." And with that, the three had a good laugh and Todd left the store.

Todd had the day to himself. Kim was at the store until closing. It was funny that just a week ago, Todd didn't even factor Kim's schedule into his own. Chuck and Trish were going to get away to Ocracoke Island for the remainder of the weekend, their favorite place to get away. So Todd went home and whiled the day away watching college football. Jack spent the day down at the beach with the neighborhood kids.

Chapter 16.

The next day's Tropical Update: Hairy Bob once again filled the TV screen. The Hurricane Hunters have flown into the storm and have extrapolated a barometric pressure of 919 millibars; this was the lowest pressure ever measured by reconnaissance aircraft over the Northern Atlantic Ocean. There also turned out to be no significant difference in the flight level winds and the surface winds, which were peaking out at 155 MPH. Izzy was now a Category 4 storm on the Saffir-Simpson scale. Its eye diameter was a very compact eight miles, and it was located about 930 miles southeast of Cape Hatteras, North Carolina. The National Hurricane Center had now issued a hurricane watch stretching from Edisto Beach, South Carolina to Cape Henry, Virginia.

Todd had a feeling that Izzy was going to turn into something nine days ago when she wasn't even named yet, back when she was just a tropical wave off the coast of Africa. He didn't know why he knew; he just knew that he did. Maybe it was the law of averages. It had been a number of years since the Outer Banks had been hit by a storm like this. "Maybe we were just due," he thought.

Todd knew that once people woke up for the day and switched on the news, the mad rush to the hardware and grocery stores would be on. People owning private residences and businesses alike would clean the hardware store out of plywood; they would need to screw the boards into their window frames to protect their windows from breaking. There would also be a scarcity of batteries, flashlights, bottled water, and canned goods. Since Todd had hurricane shutters over his windows and a generator for the house, he needed fewer of these things. So off to the store he went.

Before doing so, Todd spent the time to call each member of his crew to let each of them know about the storm and to give them a head start on the rush that was soon to hit. He also let them know that it was unlikely that there would be work the next couple of days. He requested that once they and their families were secure, either tonight or tomorrow morning, that they report to their respective job sites as a team-- at the Hyatt and the Rodanthe House-- to secure whatever needed to be secured. They all thanked him for the call and agreed they would work out amongst themselves when they could take care of their job sites.

Todd still had things to do. Besides getting his own supplies, he needed to secure the shop. Unlike his house that sat on stilts, the shop sat on level ground. He'd need to go down there and move everything from the first floor to the second. He was glad, now, that when constructing the shop, he had built the ramp for that very purpose. There would be front end loaders, mowers, and trailers to move upstairs, along with tillers, back pack blowers, and other tools and foliage.
But there was still more to be done. He knew he'd have to make sure that Kim would have the supplies she needed to ride the storm out. He'd rather she rode it out with him, where he knew she would be safe, but he also knew she would never do that. She lived in the house she grew up in near downtown Manteo, and she would never abandon it for a storm.

Then there was Chuck and Trish's house. They were out on Ocracoke Island. Would they be evacuating today or staying until they were supposed to leave on Monday? Todd would try to call Chuck, but he knew it would be fruitless --when Chuck and Trish went away for a long weekend, they would go completely off the grid. "Better I go over and take care of their house, just in case," he thought.

He came back to his house and dropped off his supplies. There he found Jack, waiting happily, and wanting to go along for the day. They say animals can sense changes in atmospheric pressure ahead of the storm, and Jack was behaving a bit needy today. It was almost like he could sense something was about to happen. There was no room in the bed of the truck where he normally rides, so Todd opened the door to the passenger side, and Jack jumped into the cab.

"Ok Ol' Boy. Gonna be a long day. Let's hit it," Todd said to Jack as he backed out of his driveway and turned towards the shop.

Once at the shop, Todd let Jack out of the truck. Jack seemed confused that they were there alone. Typically, there were always guys hanging around who would play with him and pet him. Today it was just him and Todd, and with so much work to be done, there was no time for playing.
Todd started moving everything upstairs: first there was the heavy equipment, then the smaller stuff, and finally there was the assorted foliage that was ready to go into both work sites. In his haste to move everything, he mixed them up. "Oh well," he thought, "we'll figure out what plant goes to which job site later." It was something that would have made him upset if one of his guys had done it, since he was such a stickler for details, but for now, there were more important things to tend to.

A couple of hours later and coming up on noon, Todd headed back into the truck with Jack. His next stop would be Kim's. He knew that unless she was checking the surf report, it was unlikely that she would know about the hurricane watches that had been posted. Since she worked nearly a 12-hour day yesterday, it was unlikely that she'd be going surfing today.

As Todd left the shop, he called Kim to let her know he was headed her way.

"Well, Mr. Richards. Two phone calls from you in three days. I do believe I'm growing on you again," was how she answered.

Todd, not wanting to be goaded into that conversation, merely responded, "Hey punk, see the weather report yet? Hurricane watches have been posted."

"Now, Todd. Don't be silly. You know I'm not heading out to surf today. Why would I have even looked at the weather?"

"I figured as much. I have supplies for you. Should be there in about 20 minutes."

"OK, I'll have the coffee ready."

Once there, Jack jumped out of the truck and ran to Kim. It was as if he was seeing a long-lost friend. Kim and Jack always got along great. In fact, during one of their many breakups, Todd thought that Kim missed Jack more than she missed him.

Kim's house was built in the 1960's when her parents moved off the beach and onto the island. It was closer to the Wanchese Harbor, where Kim's dad was a commercial fisherman. The house, though small and tidy, didn't have the modern storm amenities like Todd's. So, Todd spent the better part of several hours cutting and screwing plywood into the window frames. All the while, Kim was at his side. Once he was finished and the supply of bottled water and canned goods were taken inside, Todd asked Kim to please come over and ride out the storm with him.

"Oh, big tough man afraid to be by himself without his little Kimmie to protect him" is how she responded.

He knew talking to her would be futile, but he repeated that he believed she'd be safer.

"No, this is my house. I'll be perfectly fine right here. But thank you for your concern. It's kinda, oh... what's the word? Cute!"

Todd finally agreed. No one was going to ever tell Kim what to do. It seemed pointless to spend any more time on the subject. Besides, he still had to get to Chuck's to secure his place.

"I don't suppose you've heard from your brother today?"

"No, you know they go off the grid when they get away. Why?"

"Well, someone has to secure their house. I guess I'll run over there now."

Kim decided that she'd go over with him. As it turned out, it wasn't that big of a job. Chuck had the hurricane shutters for the house; they just needed to be lowered. He also had a generator. Todd started that up and let it run, and then he topped off the tank. The hardest part of the job was securing all the pool furniture and the grill. Chuck had a storage area under the house, so Todd stuck most of it in there and inside the enclosed, outside shower.

Finally finished, Todd looked jealously at Jack. All the while that Kim and he had been moving furniture, Jack decided to cool off in the pool. "Who said dogs aren't smarter than people?" Right at that moment, Kim walked by and, not knowing what possessed him, Todd threw her into the pool and then jumped in right after. They had a good laugh, and then Todd turned serious. "I'd really feel much better if you rode out the storm at my house," he said to Kim.

"Don't be silly. I'll be fine at home. We're not even sure the storm is heading this way."

After drying off, they popped open a beer they got out of Chuck's refrigerator. They put the cover on the pool, and they filled Trish's car with gas, which was left behind in the garage. Then they filled up Kim's Jeep and ran over to the Roanoke Island Outfitters Group store to bring in all the kayaks and paddle boards that were sitting outside. Since there was no second floor there, like there was at Todd's shop, all they could do was hope that the flooding would not be a factor as far inland as Highway 64. If there was flooding this far back from the sounds that surround the island, well, then there would be much bigger problems to deal with than just flooded inventory. They then lowered the hurricane shutters and called the store secure. Finally, they took Jack back to Kim's and headed out for a quick bite of dinner.

They both ordered a steak and a red wine and had an enjoyable dinner. "No pressure," Todd thought. He dropped her off at home, picked up Jack, and turned his truck towards Kitty Hawk and home.

Todd knew that the storm was too far off yet to hit tonight or anytime tomorrow, so he wasn't necessarily worried about Kim's safety or Chuck's house. He just hoped Chuck was going to make it off Ocracoke Island and onto the ferry before service was halted due to the weather. If he was coming back tomorrow, Chuck should be ok.

Both Todd and Jack were exhausted. Todd didn't notice at first that Jack had jumped into bed with him; it was so uncharacteristic. Jack always slept out on the deck, especially this time of year. "Maybe there was something to this thing about animals sensing the weather ahead of time," he thought.

Chapter 17.

"Red skies in the morning, sailors take warning...." That was exactly what Todd and Jack woke up to. It wasn't unexpected. Even if the storm didn't make a direct hit on the Outer Banks, the likelihood of getting a lot of rain was still high.

Todd went downstairs to the outside shower, grabbed a cup of coffee, and turned on the TV just as the tropical update was about to start. Todd felt more comfortable getting the news on the storm from Char. For some reason, he trusted her more than he did Hairy Bob.

The hurricane watch that had been posted from Edisto Beach, South Carolina to Cape Henry, Virginia had been elevated to a hurricane warning. The storm now seemed eminent. Landfall was expected in the next 18-24 hours. The Governor of North Carolina had just posted a voluntary evacuation of the coast from south of Wilmington to the North Carolina - Virginia border. State officials implemented lane reversing, which essentially doubles the lanes available for evacuating traffic.

Just as Todd saw the news, his phone rang. It was Chuck; they were safe and in line at the ferry to get off the island. Todd told him that he and Kim had secured the house, the pool, the store, and that they had filled up Trish's car the night before, so they didn't have to do anything except drive safely back home. Todd knew it would be several hours before Chuck would make it back since there would be a lot of people-- residents and tourists alike-- heading for safety.

Next Todd figured he better call Kim and let her know about the watch being upgraded to a warning, and that her brother, Chuck, and sister-in-law, Trish, were also aware of the storm and were in the process of making the mandatory evacuation from Ocracoke Island. It also wouldn't hurt to ask her one last time to ride out the storm in Kitty Hawk with him.

"Hey punk. Why you waking me up so early?" Kim answered.

"The watch has become a warning now. The entire Outer Banks and all of North Carolina is bracing for a hit. Is there anything you need to get you through the next couple of days?"

"No, I don't think so. What are you doing today?"

"I need to call the guys and make sure they were able to get out to both the Rodanthe House and the Hyatt job sites. I'll check in with you later."

Next Todd called each job's supervisor to find out if their crew had secured their site. The supervisor of each job indicated they had their crews working now to do just that. "Ok," Todd said. "Just don't worry about doing any actual work other than securing things. It's likely whatever you try to do will just be ripped out by the storm anyway. Get home safely to your families."

As he hung up each call, Todd was filled with gratitude for having such a great group of guys. A lot of business owners complain about their employees, but Todd considered himself lucky to be working with such conscientious people.

"Nothing to do now," Todd thought, so he pointed his truck south to the Rodanthe House. He figured he would bring his crew some coffee and sandwiches. He knew these guys would be finished before the Hyatt job.

Once the winds started pumping, it would be difficult to cross the very exposed Herbert C. Bonner Bridge that spans Oregon Inlet connecting the northern and southern Outer Banks. Todd found it ironic that the inlet he was crossing was formed when a hurricane smashed into the Outer Banks back in 1846.

As Todd was heading south, most of the traffic was heading north, evacuating from places like Ocracoke Island, Hatteras Village, and even from Rodanthe. Thankfully, he thought, most of the tourists at this time of year are only here on weekends. Since it was Monday, it made it a bit easier to evacuate.

Todd got to the Rodanthe job site and was impressed by what he found. His crew was in the finishing stages of getting everything secured. He distributed the sandwiches and coffee that he got at the nearby Hardee's. Todd spent about an hour helping to get things finished up and then told each of his crew to keep themselves and their families safe. "Obviously, with the storm due to hit sometime in the overnight hours and continuing into the next day, we won't be working tomorrow," he told the crew. "Likely won't be working Wednesday either. Take that day to get your own houses in order because, in addition to making the deadline for the two big jobs that we're currently on, you can bet we're going to be even busier with the untold amount of work we're going to get cleaning up yards for people after the storm."

"Stay safe guys," Todd repeated as he eased his truck into the northward bound traffic to make his way to the Duck - Corolla border to get to the Hyatt. Traffic was horrendous heading in this direction. Some of it eased as they got to Whalebone Junction; some of the traffic veered off there to cross the Manteo - Nags Head Causeway and off onto the mainland via the Mashoes and Stumpy Point area.

Todd stayed on the Beach Road, most everyone else took the 158 Bypass. Even though the speed limit on the Bypass was much faster, sometimes it was easier to take the slower Beach Road as there was less traffic. Today, that was certainly the case.

Todd stopped at the Hardee's in Kill Devil Hills because he knew there would be no fast food places once he got into the Southern Shores, Duck, and Corolla areas. He loaded up again with coffee and sandwiches and made his way again down the Beach Road. As he drove past the Black Pelican, at around Milepost 4, he knew that the very road he was now driving on would very likely be washed away by this time tomorrow. This stretch of road was always in peril, even during a stiff Nor'easter, let alone a hurricane. According to "the folly of man," people always think they can rebuild it better. But in the end, Mother Nature always wins. There used to be approximately a half dozen houses on the beach in this stretch, but every one of them has been washed out to sea in one storm or another.

Once Todd got into Southern Shores, traffic was much better heading north; everyone else was heading south towards Kitty Hawk to get off the Outer Banks and onto the mainland at Point Harbor and Harbinger, as they made their way to either the Elizabeth City or the Tidewater, Virginia areas. Todd got to the Hyatt just as the crew was putting the finishing touches on securing everything. He wondered how the newly planted palms would weather the storm. They hadn't really had a chance to take root into the ground just yet. "May have been a lot of work for no reason," he thought. "Just the nature of the beast when you live and work where storms like this are frequent."

When both the food and work were complete, Todd gave the same directions that he gave to his guys in Rodanthe. "Stay safe, don't worry about work on Wednesday, attend to your own affairs, and we'll reassess things on Thursday. We may be working some six or seven day weeks for the next couple of weeks."

With that, Todd was off as he mentally went through his checklist of what needed to be done prior to the storm. He did a lot of driving today, so hopefully he'd find gas somewhere along the way on his way back home. It wouldn't hurt to have a full tank of gas.

As Todd drove south, the traffic was heavy, but it was not as bad as he thought it would be. People were making their way down past Southern Shores to the turn-off to the bridge, which took them to the mainland just north of Kitty Hawk. Most people who were going to leave had already made their way off the barrier islands. Most of the people he knew, the locals of course, decided to wait out the storm in the comfort of their own homes. The danger wasn't necessarily from the force of the hurricane winds, as most of the houses down here had been constructed to withstand that. The danger was from the rising flood waters that you couldn't do anything about. If your house was built on the ground and not on stilts, you had more to worry about. Business owners had the same worry. Most of the businesses were built on the ground. The grocery stores, the hardware stores, the souvenir shops, and most of the restaurants were particularly susceptible to the rising waters of any storm.

The Outer Bankers were a stout group of people. They had survived through many storms throughout the years. Unless they were given an official mandate to leave their houses, boats, and businesses, they were not going to leave. Even then, some of these people still wouldn't leave.

Fortunately, good news was being reported on the radio! Just about an hour ago, with the latest hurricane update, the National Hurricane Center said the worst of the hurricane was expected to stay offshore. This allowed the Outer Banks to collectively breathe a huge sigh of relief.

Todd looked at the time. It was just after 3 pm. He knew the storm was likely to be a little less than 12 hours away. For whatever reason, hurricanes always have the propensity to strike when it's dark, which makes it even a little spookier when you can't see the thing that's attacking you.
Due to cooler water temperatures, Hurricanes, as a rule, generally lose power and strength after going north of Florida. And for a time, Izzy did lose power, dropping from a major hurricane to a Category 2 storm as her winds dropped to 96 MPH. Izzy had other ideas. She apparently decided she wasn't going to be a typical hurricane, so she actually strengthened as she tracked northward over the Gulf Stream -- the powerful, warm, and swift Atlantic Ocean current that originates in the Gulf of Mexico and stretches to the tip of Florida, following the eastern coastlines of the United States and Newfoundland before crossing the Atlantic Ocean. Its presence has led to the development of strong cyclonic conditions of all types, both in the atmosphere and within the ocean. Izzy apparently decided to take full advantage of the warm temperature of the waters. Todd decided to dwell on the good news. As long as she stayed on that northerly pattern, everything would be alright; most of the storm would stay offshore.

As Todd was nearing home, he wondered if Jack attempted to get out to the beach today. "Likely he hadn't," Todd thought. "The water was already getting too rough."

Todd turned into his driveway, pulled the truck underneath the house, and saw that Jack was up on the deck waiting for him. Together they walked over to the sound side of the pier to check out Mother Nature's doings. As they got there, the winds were picking up as the storm inched closer and closer. There were already whitecaps on the sound, and that was not an everyday occurrence here. Typically, the sound is pretty calm and flat, but today it was getting angrier and angrier.

"No ball throwing today Ol' Boy," Todd murmured to Jack.

"No doubt you'd be able to do it, but at your age, you'd only be good for one trip. Then you'd be all wet and sandy while we'd be cooped up in the house together."

Yes, Jack wasn't Todd's dog. In the strictest sense he didn't live with Todd, but there was no way that Todd wasn't going to bring him in during this storm. The mere fact that no one from the neighborhood had brought Jack in made it clear that everyone knew that Todd would take care of him.

"Come on boy. Let's go call that pig-headed girl over there on the island. Let's see if she'll change her mind about keeping us company during this storm."

Todd and Jack walked back to the house. No one else was out. Everyone's hurricane shutters were starting to close, and there were several hurricane parties going on as well. He and Jack were invited to each party that they passed, but Todd declined each of the invitations. Todd was always amazed by those things. Whenever there was a huge storm coming, people would party and drink themselves into a stupor. Now Todd enjoyed having a beer or three, but he always thought it more prudent to have your wits about you should you need them in an emergency during a storm.

Todd got home, lowered his hurricane shutters, and remembered he forgot to get gas on his way home. "Better to get it now," he thought, "in case there will be no serviceable pumps after the storm comes rumbling through." He had Ocean 105 on the radio and during their hurricane coverage, they mentioned that the Shell station at the Outer Banks Mall still had gas and was open for business until sundown.

"Come on Jack. Let's take a last ride before Izzy gets here." With that, Jack jumped into his usual spot in the bed of the truck. "You really want to sit back there boy? Getting to be a bit breezy out. Rain is likely to start before we get home."

Jack didn't budge. He just looked at Todd and panted as if to say, "Come on dude. Let's get this show on the road." And with that, they were off down the Bypass to the Shell Station.

Todd had the slider on the back of the truck open as he decided to call Kim to make one last ditch effort at having her evacuate her house and come out to Kitty Hawk with him, where he knew it would be safer.

"No, Todd. I'll be fine. Chuck just called. He said he'd be home in about 15 minutes, and they're just down the street if I need anything."

"You sure are a stubborn little wench Kim. Just promise me that you'll stay inside and call me if you need anything while the cell service is still up."

She promised she would and hung up as Todd pulled into the gas station. While he was here, he decided to gas up and run inside and grab a few snacks to occupy his time while waiting for the storm to pass.

As he expected, there wasn't much left on the shelves. The place looked like it was going out of business; it was so empty. Todd did find some Doritos and a can of bean dip. He laughed to himself as he walked up to the counter to pay for his purchases. "I came for gas, and gas I shall have."

Todd walked back outside to his truck. The wind was blowing a bit harder. The rain was starting to come down and the skies were a more ominous gray than he'd ever seen before. "You might want to think about closing up," he called back to the kid at the counter. "Gonna start getting nasty soon."

As Todd got to his truck, he was amazed to find that Jack was missing. "Gone! He's never run off before, and now, this time, of all times!" It was starting to get dark and the storm was only hours away.

Todd searched. He drove the truck up one side street down to the sound and then up another side street down to the ocean. He got out of the truck, every so often, and called out for Jack, listening intently for any sound from him. The wind was gaining strength and howling, probably close to gale force by now, and Todd could barely hear his own voice, so it was doubtful that it could be heard down the street or through a yard. But they say dogs can hear so much better than humans, so who knows? The rain was coming down almost sideways, and it was getting darker by the minute. The streets were abandoned, so there was no one to elicit any help from. Still, Todd continued to look. The problem was that at this point, Jack could literally be a couple of miles away down any number of side streets and holed up underneath someone's house or even on their deck right next door to where Todd was standing. There was just no way of knowing.

After what seemed like hours, Todd simply had to give up, head home, and hope that Jack would be ok. There were other animals out there in this storm that didn't have shelter. Animals like birds, and squirrels, and fox. If they could make it, there was no reason to believe that Jack couldn't either. Still, Jack wasn't a wild animal who was used to surviving every day on his own. This was a dog that had become accustomed to being fed and having a warm and safe place to sleep every night. He was not an animal that had been forced to survive by its wits, until now.

Reluctantly, Todd headed for home. They say animals always know their way home. Maybe Jack had become disorientated at the beginning of the storm and decided to head for home. Todd wasn't at the truck when he left; he was inside buying snacks. Maybe Jack thought Todd was the one that disappeared.

Trying to remain hopeful, Todd drove home as quickly as he could. Other than a few other cars out for a sightseeing ride to see what it looked like before the storm, Todd was the only one on the roads, and he wasn't paying attention to the speed limits. Knowing that Jack couldn't cover the distance as quickly as the truck, Todd kept his eyes on the road, sweeping from side to side, looking for a yellow lab out walking by himself. But he had no luck finding him.

By the time Todd got back home, there were no sightings of Jack at all—not on the road and not on the deck. Todd immediately ran upstairs and raised the Hurricane shutter on the door leading to the deck from the bedroom. That would be the deck that Jack would come back home to, so Todd would leave it open for as long as it was safe to do so.

Todd called Kim and explained the situation to her. She was as reassuring as she could be.

She knew that Jack was the one thing that kept Todd sane when she was causing him undue stress during those off again portions of their on-again and off-again relationship. Todd would never come out and say it, of course, but she knew that Todd loved that dog more than anything. She told Todd that Jack was smart and would make his way back home before the storm fully hit. Animals have a sixth sense about those things. She also let Todd know that she talked to Chuck and that both he and Trish had made it home safely and were very appreciative of everything Todd and Kim had done to prepare their home and store for the storm. She promised that she would call Chuck now to let him know about Jack, and that as soon as she was able to get out after the storm, she would come over to the beach to help look for Jack, should he have not made it back home by then.

The lights began to flicker and Todd asked Kim one more time if she was ok being there alone. She said she was and with that, they each wished each other good luck and promised to check in with each other in a bit.

"Great!" Todd said to himself. "Not enough that I have to worry about her. Now I also have to worry about that damn mangy mutt."

Todd flipped on the Weather Channel, and even though it was way past the time she would normally be on the air, Char was at her post looking very worn out after what must have been a very long and tiring day.

What was being reported was very alarming. The storm was going to hit at a time that coincided with the highest lunar tide of the year! That meant the damage was likely to be extensive. However, as long as it continued tracking on that straight northerly track, the devastation would be minimized.

More news was coming in. A buoy, about 60 miles east of the center, recorded a wave height of 48 feet, making it the highest buoy wave recorded in an Atlantic hurricane, ever.

As the winds continued to howl and the rain continued to pelt the hurricane shutters and the exposed glass of the deck door, Todd continued to keep a lookout for Jack, as he was hopefully making his way home. Todd was tempted to go back out into the storm to make one last attempt at finding the dog, but he knew it would be futile. It was pitch black outside and the rain was coming down so hard that Todd wouldn't be able to see past the hood of the truck. Besides, he had no idea where to even start to look!

Todd couldn't sit. Todd wasn't much of a sitter. He was more of a pacer by nature, and he was certainly wearing a path into the hardware floors with his constant back and forth movement.

Suddenly the lights were flickering again, and it was only a matter of time before he would be in complete darkness and would have to start his generator. Just as he was thinking that, his concentration was snapped by an immediate update on the position of the storm. It seemed that Izzy was playing hardball. She was coming to town, and she wasn't going to be nice about it. The latest reports had her taking a sudden sharp northwest turn and heading for land! The eye had widened considerably to 25 miles and was churning towards the southern end of the Outer Bank. She was expected to make landfall in the overnight hours. Her winds were now clocked at about 130 MPH, or a Category 4 on the Saffir-Simpson scale.

Twelve days ago, this was nothing more than a tropical wave in some far off place on the other side of the ocean. Now she was a full fledged, angry ass storm with a name, and she was coming straight after him.

Todd, who normally doesn't panic in intense situations, reached for his cell phone to call Kim. "Hey, how you doing over there on the island?" He asked as she answered the phone.

"What? This lil' ol' spring shower? Gonna take more than that to scare this native Outer Banker you dirty Yankee! Any news about Jack yet?"

"No. I have no idea why he would have run off like that. Maybe he got spooked. I don't know. I just hope he's ok."

"Yeah, he will be. Remember, Jack was born here. That makes him an Outer Banker. And if it's one thing we Outer Bankers know, it's how to survive and thrive. And look at the bright side, in a couple of days, the waves will be pumping again, and you know how Jack loves to body surf next to me as I'm riding a wave."

"Yeah, you're right," said Todd, smiling at the mental image that conjured up. "He's a smart dog. He'll be ok. You did see the latest, right? It's going to hit us smack in the face sometime tonight."

"Yeah, I saw. We'll be fine. You, me, and Jack. We'll all be fine. I'll check in with you again in a little bit. Try not to worry."

"I'll try. We'll probably lose cell service a couple of hours out ahead of the storm so don't wait too long before checking back in."

"I won't. I promise. Oh, Todd?"

"Yeah?"

"Thanks for caring about me."

"Anytime. Besides, I need someone who will change my diapers when I get older," he chuckled, "so I have to stay on your good side."

"Way to ruin a moment, ass! Bye."

With that, the lights flickered one last time and went out. Todd sat there for a few moments in the dark thinking back on things. He thought about how he and Kim first met out at the Avalon Pier surfing one bright, sunny Mid-August afternoon a few years ago. Todd thought about the time he found this little stray yellow lab sleeping on his deck --the place he's slept every night since, up until tonight. Life for him had changed since moving down here. His brother Bryant and his wife Jill were back in Ohio. They had three kids now who were all grown, and who all loved spending time with their Uncle Todd down at the beach; the uncle with no family, but lots of cool toys-- surfboards, stand up paddle boards, boogie boards and kayaks. It was everything a kid could want.

"That's all well and good," Todd thought. "But I best crank up the generator to get some lights back on and keep the refrigerator running, and I better keep an eye on the weather channel until the cable goes out, which likely will be soon."

Todd got up, started the generator, and soon thereafter, there was power to the house again. He again, stepped out on the deck to check one last time for any signs of Jack. "Poor thing. He must be miserable," he said out loud as the wind deafened all sound.

The weather was getting worse. There had to be enough wind at this point to equal tropical force strength as the outer bands of the storm started making their way to the shore. These were dangerous areas of hurricanes. Tornadoes often spawn in these outer bands, and Todd had no doubt that tornado warnings were now posted.

In fact, they were. That was the latest from the weather channel. It was time to close that last shutter. Todd was very reluctant to do so, but knew he had to now; things were getting way too dicey to chance keeping it open any longer. So, he lowered that shutter slowly as he looked for any last minute miracle of a dog walking up the driveway without a care in the world.

With the last shutter now finally closed, Todd sat down to watch whatever new shred of news he could find about Izzy. He knew there wouldn't be any information that he himself couldn't provide. By the time the next update would come through, the storm will have made landfall and the cable would be out. There may be a chance that Ocean 105 could still be on the air, but they would only be able to report what they could see out their own studio window, or what the police could see out their windows and relay to them via the shortwave. No one would be venturing out into this weather until Izzy blew, both figuratively and literally, out of town. Winds now approached hurricane strength as the storm inched closer and closer to landfall.

"It's looking like Hatteras Village will be the spot where Izzy meets the land --the point where the initial destruction will take place. If she wobbles to the right, she keeps most of her strength out at sea.

If she wobbles to the left and then tracks up the Pamlico Sound into the Albemarle Sound of the North Carolina coast, she'll maintain or even increase her power as she's being fed by the warm shallow waters. Nothing to do but wait till the end now," Todd thought.

Over in Manteo on Roanoke Island, Kim also had a combination of the Weather Channel and Ocean 105 on trying to keep abreast of the weather situation. She also knew that she wouldn't learn any new information from the two sources but just had it on for a comforting effect. The house was dark with the hurricane shutters screwed into place and the lights flickered more and more. She knew it was only a matter of time before she'd be in total darkness as the island would surely lose power soon. But she was ready. She had her supply of candles and her lighter. She knew there would likely be no sleeping tonight and planned to wile the hours away reading a book by candlelight, a' la Abraham Lincoln.

Just as she was about to settle into a comfortable position on the couch, Kim heard a strange scratching sound at the back door. At first she tried to ignore it, thinking it was a raccoon or some other type of animal trying to find a warm, dry spot from the storm. The scratching was incessant. There was a "I'm not going to give up until you come out and see what I am" kind of scratching.

Kim, very reluctantly and very slowly, opened the back door to try and locate the source of the noise. The hurricane strengthened winds made it very difficult, but when she finally was able to crack the door open, a big blur of fast, wet fur came crashing into the house.

It ran past Kim and darted through the kitchen and into the living room. Now Kim was scared. She had no idea what the hell just made itself a resident in her home. Was it a dangerous animal, like one of the swamp foxes, or some sort of bobcat that may have gotten lost in the storm and was disoriented? Kim didn't know but wasn't too excited about investigating either.

Just then, the blur of fur came back in her direction and jumped up on her with enough force to knock her to the ground.

She stayed there stunned for a moment and then started to laugh, uncontrollably. "Jack, you son-of-a-bitch! She yelled. "You just scared the crap out of me! What are you doing here? Todd has been worried sick about you I'm sure. We better call him to let him know you're safe."

With that, Kim grabbed her cellphone and dialed Todd's number. She knew he would answer the call because he'd be worried about her and because she told him she'd check in again.

Todd's phone rang and through the static he answered. "Hey Kim, everything ok?"

"Yeah, babe. In fact, I have a visitor that decided to ride the storm out with me."

"Oh yeah, who's……" and with that, the cell towers went down.

"Well, that's it," Todd thought. "Cell phones are down. Cable and radio are the next to go."

Todd was troubled by the fact he wouldn't be able to make sure that Kim was safe through the storm, but he was glad she had someone there with her. It was likely her surfing friend, Kallie. Kallie also lived on the Island in one of the apartments above the bookstore downtown, just down the street from Kim. She probably got freaked out and decided to bunk in with Kim for the night. He was glad she had the company.

The Weather Channel had people reporting up and down the east coast. Each one called this the "Storm of the Century," as they do with every storm it seems.

"Doesn't seem mathematically possible that every storm can be called that," Todd chuckled to himself.

He remembered when snow dumped all of eight inches on Cleveland last winter in one overnight blast that was dubbed "Snowmageddon." "Really?!?" He knew from experience that eight inches in Cleveland was a minor disturbance at best, not something that needed to be compared to the end of the world.

He reckoned that the media did whatever they had to do to create viewership and keep their advertisers happy, but it did a great disservice to those in the direct path of the storm. It was much better to keep things realistic rather than to over inflate the importance of what was happening. The problem now is that every storm was bigger and badder than the last, so the weather service had created a "boy cries wolf" situation. When the real "Storm of the Century" hits, people will be used to not paying attention to the hyperbole and innocent lives will be lost.

"Is tonight really the 'Storm of the Century' or just another ploy to keep the Weather Channel advertisers happy? I guess we'll know in the next few hours."

According to the weather reporters, Izzy was just a couple of hours away from making landfall. With her current track, it seemed like Hatteras Village would be the impact point.

Sustained winds were clocking in at 119 MPH, dropping from 130, as she lost some steam heading northwest. That was the reading from The Diamond Shoal Light, located offshore a short while ago. Gusts had reached 132 MPH.

The strongest of those winds were located on the eastern periphery of the storm, which in turn meant reduced winds over land. But 119 MPH was nothing to sneeze at either. This still made her a Category 3 storm and according to the Saffir-Simpson scale, a Cat 3 storm is defined as:

Devastating damage will occur: Well-built framed homes may incur major damage or removal of roof decking and gable ends. Many trees will be snapped or uprooted, blocking numerous roads. Electricity and water will be unavailable for several days to weeks after the storm passes.

As Hurricane Izzy inched closer and closer to Hatteras Village, her outer edges began to incorporate the air over the land and transferred them in towards her eye. Since that air was much cooler and drier than the warm, moist air fueling the storm, heavy thunderstorms and tornadoes were birthed as the storm surge, made even larger by the high lunar tide cycle, started to come ashore. Rains had been pelting Hatteras Village for several hours now, and the much-anticipated storm surge was now predicted to cause extensive flooding for the area.

"It's not the initial surge that is often the worst. It's the secondary flow of water that can be devastating," the weather anchor explained. "As the rain and surge fill up the Pamlico Sound behind the southern Outer Banks, her outlets will likely get clogged up by debris pushed up by high waves causing new inlets in the barrier beaches for the water to escape."
All of this science was likely to repeat itself further north as Izzy made her way north into the Albemarle Sound.

The meteorologists of the world describe landfall of a hurricane as being when the eye of the storm crosses from the water over the land. The image of this can be seen on satellite images and on radar. Todd thought this was a lousy way to record things. The hurricane had already struck, as far as the people in the line of the storm were concerned, here on the Outer Banks. They had already been experiencing torrential downpours of rain and hurricane force winds for hours. Science says that Izzy hasn't struck land yet due to the eye still being out at sea. And if her eye continues to wobble over water and not land, she will not have officially made landfall at all. Try telling the people in Hatteras Village that she never made it to shore. They'll have a different story to tell. The storm surge had probably already started causing major beach erosion and had likely caused some houses on the beach to be compromised.

And with that, the TV went black and the cable was out. Frankly, Todd was surprised it had lasted this long. Ocean 105 was now the sole eyes and ears for those on the Outer Banks. The staff at the radio station was all there. It didn't matter whose air shift this was supposed to be; all hands were on deck.

The general manager was the lone person in communication with the National Weather Service, while the news director was in constant touch with both the police and fire departments. Both of them were handing off whatever information they had to the staff of radio announcers that were not currently on the air, and then that group would hand it off to the person who was. The sales team kept the coffee going and helped where they could. They were the ones in communication with the governor's office in Raleigh. Suddenly, this tiny radio station, carved out in the swamp in Wanchese on the south end of Roanoke Island, was the epicenter for communications on this storm. It was going to be a long night.

Flooding was already occurring down south and there were reports that a portion of Highway 12 was washed out at the S Curves, just north of Rodanthe. Rains were coming down and the flood waters were coming up as Izzy continued to blow and make her way towards land. The "Storm of the Century," or not, this was going to be a hell of a ride for all concerned on the Outer Banks of North Carolina. It was a place that just a few days ago was a tourist paradise, a place for others to own and operate their businesses, and a place for families to call home. Now it stood in direct sight of an angry woman named Izzy. What did they collectively do to cause the ire of such an angry, merciless spawn of Mother Nature?

As the minutes passed, it started to feel like hours. There was nothing new from the radio other than the news about more rain, more surges, more flooding, more winds, and the expectation of severe and extensive damage.

The flood waters were moving further and further north up the Pamlico and into the Albemarle. Ocean 105, which sits just off the shores of the sound separated by only about 100 yards of swamp, was in danger of being flooded. Soon the waters would be creeping up the walls of the station. The governor and the fire department agreed that the tiny station had to pull the plug. She performed admirably in the days and hours leading up to Izzy making landfall, but now, for the safety of all the staff, they had to abandon ship. The problem was that the waters had already started to rise and the employees had no way out.

The Roanoke Island Volunteer Fire Department had no other choice than to crank up their patrol boat and cruise into the station on a road that cars once drove on. After three trips, all of the staff were safely evacuated out of the station. The last two staffers, the general manager and the news director, perched themselves up on the roof due to the rising waters and held on to whatever they could to keep from being blown off.

"Well, that's all she wrote," Todd thought. There were no cell phones, no TV, and now, no radio. All communication from the outside world had ceased to exist, and little did he know, but at this exact second, Izzy came ashore in Hatteras Village.

Todd's thoughts were divided between two living beings: Kim was the first. "Was she ok through all this?" And then there was Jack. "Where in the hell was that bastard?" Part of him was consumed with anger that Jack would just disappear.

A bigger part of him was worried. He worried about whether Jack was safe and mostly dry.

Jack was a yellow lab and by nature they are superior swimmers, but this was another ball game altogether. This wasn't a calm and serene sound. These were raging waters created by one hell of a storm. Whitecaps, usually reserved for the ocean, were no doubt now also located on the town's side streets, where cars once drove and kids once played.

Chapter 18.

Izzy made landfall in the wee hours of the morning, one a.m. local time. A high tide came ahead of her just before midnight; the high lunar tide is the highest tide of the lunar year.

Of course, Todd couldn't know that as he sat in the dim light that was kept running by a generator. Izzy, when her eye made landfall, had winds that were walloping the little coastal town measuring at 115 MPH. That put her as a Category 3 storm, which is still classified as a major hurricane. She was tracking north and was going to take the path right up the coastal sounds. Typically, at the time a hurricane's eye crosses the coast, the inflowing wind speed has decreased due to the cooler, drier air moving in, which results in a rapid weakening of the storm. But Izzy had been and would remain atypical; she was not your normal storm. She maintained her strength and decided to hitch a ride on the gulf stream. She was not typical when she took a sudden turn to the west when her eye was expected to stay out to sea. Why would anyone expect her to not keep fueling herself with the warm, moist waters of both Pamlico and Albemarle Sounds?

Hatteras Village sits at the extreme southwesterly tip of Hatteras Island, approximately 70 miles south of Kitty Hawk and straight down Highway 12. The tiny village is always sitting naked against storms, exposed on the small barrier island, only three feet above sea level. With any luck, the 500 or so souls that make this their year-round home had fled ahead of the storm. That's what common sense would dictate anyway, but these people were sturdy Outer Bankers.

Most of them had weathered these kinds of storms before. Those that had, had two mindsets: either get out because the expected loss would be high, or take your chances and ride out the storm so you can be there when it's over to immediately start picking up the pieces. As it turns out, most of the people were of the latter group.

Much of Hatteras Island makes its living off of fishing. In-shore charters are available to fish the Pamlico Sound. Deep sea fishing boats are chartered out of The Hatteras Harbor Marina. From there, they take fishermen out to the warm waters of the gulf stream, located about an hour and a half out into the ocean, to catch both blue and white marlin, tuna, wahoo and mahi mahi.

Built in 1901, the Hatteras Weather Bureau Station is also located in the town. No doubt, with her instruments pointed at the storm, she is doing her best to just keep standing at the moment. Even though her duties are no longer weather related, North Carolina State University, which conducts studies on marine invertebrates at the facility, still keeps a token weather reporting station going for just such events.

As Izzy's eye comes across the land, a general calmness starts to grace the tiny village. The eye is always the calm before the next storm. The tidal surge that is typically on the eastern edge of the eye wall has already played havoc on the village with heavy, relentless rain. But those familiar with such storms know the worst was yet to play out, in spite of what seemed like a beautiful early morning hour. Once the eye totally passes, the winds will swirl in from the opposite direction. The initial winds blew all the sound water out, away from the island. But now, the water will be making a vengeful return with the winds blowing in a clockwise fashion. This will be the point when all the waters will rise and swallow everything in their path.

As Izzy was moving to the north, straight up the Pamlico Sound, a swath of devastation was left in her wake. Entire hotels were literally picked up off of their foundations and tossed aside like they were empty potato chip bags. One tourist, who had never seen a hurricane before, decided not to take the advice of the governor. Instead, she decided to witness the storm from her first floor hotel room. Luckily, she was able to climb into the attic as the hotel was picked up and started to float away. Later, after the storm, she was rescued from the attic as the water was already up to her chest. If it had been just a little longer, the water would have totally consumed her. She was one of the lucky ones. Others weren't quite so fortunate. The next morning, residents were found clinging to trees after their houses slid out from underneath them. Boats in the Hatteras Village Marina were strewn about as if a child hadn't put their toys away prior to going to bed for the night. One boat was carried nearly a half mile away and deposited on the beach, ocean-side. Another, a 30-footer, ended up sitting in the backyard pool of a home a football field away, while most of the others just sat in the marina in various stages of being swamped. Hatteras Island itself was affected. It was no longer just a single island. It was now several islands as Izzy, laughing as she made her way north to create further havoc, cut several new inlets from sound to ocean.

Just up the road in Frisco, at the Billy Mitchell Airport, the runway was totally unusable as sand, knee deep, was picked up from the beach and deposited there. It was as if Izzy was trying to say, "Yeah, try to get out now. You should have left when you had the chance."

The Cape Hatteras Lighthouse is located in Buxton. Most school aged children can describe her as the light house with the black and white spirals.

Standing at 210 feet, she is the tallest brick lighthouse structure in the United States, and she is easily the most recognizable of all of the East Coast lighthouses. It was almost like Izzy used her to find her way, as have thousands of sailors throughout the years. If she wasn't moved to her present location back in 1999, she surely would have been another victim of Hurricane Izzy. But as the storm passed over her, she remained standing in defiance of the storm that had already wrought so much damage.

Izzy's eye creeped and inched further north, passing through the coastal towns of Avon, Salvo, Waves and now Rodanthe, the eastern most point of North Carolina, and a place where they still celebrate "Old Christmas" on January 6th. The devastation was the same in all areas. The pier, so famously depicted in the movie "Nights in Rodanthe," was completely destroyed. Izzy snapped it in two without even blinking. The houses and businesses did their best to withstand the storm, but most of them lost. Whatever damage may have occurred at Todd's worksite at the Inn at Rodanthe, would have to wait to be discovered in the days ahead by its owners in the morning light. The house was still unoccupied as the work that was being done on it was still being completed. There was no doubt that much of the exterior work would have to be redone, if the house even still existed.

Highway 12, at this point, was nothing more than a sand-swept dotted line connecting one harrowing scene to another. Izzy's eye wall, more furious than she was just an hour ago, had crossed over the Pamlico Sound and was now in the Roanoke Sound, and she was still picking up warm, moist air along the way. Fish that are normally found only in the ocean waters were being picked up and deposited into the sound, into people's backyards and onto roofs of buildings. Man or animal, it didn't matter to Izzy. If you were in her way, you were going to be feeling her wrath.

As the storm's eye wall made its way to the sound, the southern part of Roanoke Island was next in her path. Izzy's presence had been felt for hours, with her outer bands bringing torrential rain and a huge storm surge as her calling card before arriving. Those same outer bands that had already chased the radio station staff out of their post, created an informational blackout for those in the path of the storm.

On the north end of the Island, Kim, protected and in the company of Jack; and Chuck and Trish all braced for the storm's fury. As they each huddled in their own homes, they expected the worst and hoped for the best. Kim lay awake in the dark listening to the snapping and popping of the tall pines that surrounded her Manteo home. Chuck and Trish experienced the same sound show, which sounded more like dynamite going off than trees toppling. The ground, already saturated from the heavy thunderstorms that preceded the eye wall, provided no stable hold for the trees.

Now, as the winds picked up in intensity, the pines blew over onto cars, fences, houses, and businesses. They had no fight left in them since the lack of root structure left them totally compromised. One particularly loud snap and pop was preceded by an even louder crashing sound as a twenty-five foot pine landed squarely on Kim's roof. She and Jack climbed the stairs to the upper level, as quickly as they could, to check on the damage. In total darkness, this was a proposition that was easier said than done. Kim carefully carried a candle with her. Once she reached the bedrooms upstairs, she held it high above her head to survey any potential damage. Thankfully, after inspecting each room, she saw no daylight through the roof nor did she notice any water getting in. Kim thought to herself that she was lucky this time and wondered what might be next, just as the next pop and snap indicated yet another falling tree.

Just a few hundred yards down the street, Chuck and Trish were experiencing the exact same scenario. Chuck also listened as the trees all around him were snapping and crashing into different structures. He was not only worried about that, but he was also concerned about the rising waters of the surge and the rain. There weren't any trees really surrounding the storefront of the Roanoke Island Outfitters Group, but it was sitting flush on the ground up on Highway 64. And if the water rose and made its way up the 3/4 of a mile from the sound to his business's front door, he would experience significant inventory loss, maybe his entire business.

However, Chuck had no inclination to close down his business and work for someone else again; he tried that before, and for whatever reason had never been able to fit into a mold of working for someone else. He just couldn't see himself spending his days doing what someone else told him to do, how to do it, and when to do it. No, he had an independent streak so wide that he never had been happy doing what he called the "sheep mentality," getting up when someone tells you to get up and spending as many hours of your life as someone tells you to spend as a mindless drone. The worst business decision, in Chuck's opinion, is one where you trade your time for money. That's what working for an hourly wage or salary amounted to, as far as Chuck was concerned.

 Todd, barricaded in his home in Kitty Hawk, didn't get any sleep either. The firecracker sound of trees snapping were not just heard on Roanoke Island, but over on the beach too. Granted, there weren't as many trees there, but there were enough to cause a significant amount of damage.

The generator was still humming along, although Todd couldn't hear it above the howling and the groaning of the winds, which still maintained a speed of well over 100 MPH. The eye wall had lost some strength as it moved forward, but the loss was not significant. Izzy would still be a dangerous storm despite reducing some of her strength. She was still capable of damaging buildings. Though the structures are built to withstand many storms, each storm has its own unique characteristics that you can't protect yourself from, and Izzy was no different. Surely there would be a lot to recover from in the days ahead. It's likely that the Outer Banks, Jeannette's, The Nags Head, Avalon. and Kitty Hawk Piers would all meet the same fate as the Rodanthe Pier. Izzy was hungry and she demanded to be fed!

Though Todd didn't want to dwell on it, he wondered how Jack could survive this storm with all of the rain, storm surge, winds, and trees falling all around. It would take a miracle for Jack to come through all of this completely unscathed. Though tempted, Todd didn't succumb to his curiosity to open one of the hurricane shutters and look at all of the damage that he heard crashing all around him. He'd have to wait until the eye came overhead.

"Why tempt fate? For a brief moment of satisfying my curiosity? After all, didn't that once kill a cat? Well, at least it wasn't a dog," he thought, as he made himself chuckle.

As the crow flies, or as a hurricane tracks, there wasn't much distance between where Kim, Chuck, and Trish were on Roanoke Island, and where Todd was in Kitty Hawk, so they all experienced the eye passing over them at pretty much the exact same time.

It would last about 15 minutes or so before the winds would pick back up again, this time going in the opposite direction. So, if there was a time to look outside, this was it. Kim stepped outside, making very sure to not open the door too wide and let Jack back out. Although it was still pitch black, as it is often darkest before the dawn, she was not ready to discover what she found. The twenty five foot pine was lying precariously on the roof of the house. There was no apparent damage, except for some shingles that would need to be replaced. She was very worried that with the way the tree was lying that the wind on the backside of the storm could pick it back up and use it as a flying missile, creating even more damage.

The flood waters were there, though not especially high yet. She knew that the potential for extensive flooding still lay in the hours ahead, when the winds come back around and push all the water back into the sound and up on shore. She looked down the street in the direction of her big brother Chuck's house. It was actually brightly lit down that way, thanks largely to the sparking electrical lines that lay on the ground.

Chuck very carefully stepped outside. There was no damage to the house, although the pool looked like it got hammered. There looked to be about three and a half feet of sand on top of the pool cover, which was straining under the weight. Although it was a saltwater pool, there was no doubt that actual saltwater from the ocean was now mixed in with the man-made kind. His inclination was to go down the road to check on the condition of his store, but the sparking electrical wires that provided the light to survey his yard and pool were the same sparking wires that prohibited him from leaving his yard.

"His livelihood wouldn't matter if he didn't have a life," he thought. He also wanted to check on Kim as he looked down their street and thought he caught a glimpse of her looking at him, but he couldn't be sure. He knew that she would know better than to go out to explore at this point of the night. It was probably best to just go back inside and hunker down for the less windy, albeit, worst part of the storm. With that, he went to the refrigerator and grabbed a beer. As he sat down on the couch next to Trish, he caught her disapproving glare.

"What?" He asked. "The generator is not going to last forever and likely will run out of gas before the power is going to be restored. I'm just finishing this beer before it goes bad. I mean, you're the one who's always yelling at me not to waste things." With that, they both laughed as the winds started back up.

While Kim and Chuck were checking out their respective homes and yards, Todd also went out to do some investigating. In fact, probably most of the people riding out the storm on the Outer Banks did the same thing. After all, residents on the Outer Banks prided themselves on ignoring evacuation orders and would often tell hurricane tales the way some people tell fish stories.

Todd opened the hurricane shutter leading from the bedroom onto the deck; he was hoping for a miracle, and that Jack would be out there in his usual spot as he was each evening, but of course, he wasn't. Todd checked under the house, under the car, and in the outside shower to see if Jack was able to get into any one of those places during the storm. Unfortunately, there was still no sign of him.

Todd was lucky when it came to the damage on his house.

Even though he sat on top of a rise, more than most of his neighbors, the winds didn't topple the large pine tree in the front of his house. Though its root structure had been compromised from the heavy rains, she was still standing. Hopefully, when the winds picked back up going in the opposite direction, she'd remain standing.

Looking down the street to the right and towards the sound, Todd saw quite a bit of destruction. The pier that Jack and he use to throw the tennis ball into the water from was gone. The spot was completely empty, so it was hard to imagine that it had ever been there in the first place. Not a single shred of timber that was used in its construction remained.

The waters of the sound looked as if they were pushed out. In fact, in the darkness by the light of sparking electrical wires, he noticed that a lot of the water was gone. When the winds whip around, they move all that water back in at once, so that's where the water from the back end of this storm would be coming from next.

Looking down the street to the left, in the direction of the ocean, he noticed significant flooding below the crest that he was on. Quite a few trees were lying across the road causing a damming effect with the water. If those trees remained there, it would increase the likelihood of the flood waters affecting his house since the street had suddenly been turned into a reservoir. Todd wanted to go down and try to move some of the debris to allow the water to flow, but he faced the exact predicament that Chuck faced – each one was contained to his own property by the fallen electrical wires. Death by electrocution did not appeal to Todd, but neither did death by drowning. He'd have to take his chances.

Now turning his attention to the house, for the most part, everything seemed pretty well buttoned up.

Most of the damage was on the roofline; some shingles were missing and the TV satellite dish came loose from its mooring. All in all, he escaped any major damage. It was just the rising waters and the dam at the end of the street that concerned him.

The neighbors across the street were also surveying their damage. Marissa and Lou were a young couple from Atlanta that had just moved to the Outer Banks back in May. This was their first hurricane ever, and they didn't quite know what to expect. Todd and the young couple waved to each other but none of them dared to cross the street in fear of the downed wires.

"Helluva storm so far," Todd yelled across the street.

"So far? You mean there's more? We thought it was over."

Todd yelled back, "Only half over. This is only the calm of the eye. There is more to come."

Visibly shaken by the news that the storm still had life to it, Marissa, who went by the nickname Riss, called back over to Todd. "But the worst part is over, right?"

"Well, I guess it depends on what you mean by the worst part," Todd yelled back. "If you mean winds, then yeah, the worst of that is over. If you mean potential destruction, then no. That's still to come."

Todd explained that most damage comes from the flooding waters left in the wake of a hurricane and how the waters of the sound were going to be rushing back in soon. It will spill over its banks and onto their street and the other surrounding streets.

To further complicate things, "see the trees lying across the road? They're going to hold a lot of that water back from rushing all the way down the crest and into the ocean. It's likely to pool up on this end of the street."

"Did we make a mistake by staying here and not evacuating?" Riss yelled out seemingly worried about their decision.

Todd yelled back across the street, "Too early to tell, but you made it this far. Ya'll will be alright. Just stay inside until the storm has completely passed and don't go wading through any standing water once it's over either. Look at the bright side. You guys are going to be busy in the coming days ahead down at your store."

Riss and Lou moved to the Outer Banks to open their own hardware store. Lou had been raised in the business having worked at his father's store his whole life. Now he had started his own. Riss's background was in accounting. She was doing all the bookkeeping and taxes for the store. There was no doubt that they would be busy once the storm was over. The locals were going to need a lot of supplies to do their repairs, and in anticipation of the storm, the young couple had over bought on those supplies to make sure they were ready for the onslaught of buyers.

"By the way," Todd yelled back across the street, "Jack is missing. You hadn't, by chance, seen him just before the storm hit, did you?"

"Oh my gosh, no! That's so sad," Riss yelled back. "He's a smart dog, though. Do you think he's safe?"

All Todd could muster was, "I don't know. I certainly hope so."

All at once, the winds started picking back up. "Time to batten down the hatches again kids," Todd yelled across the street. "Remember, the waters will be rushing in from the sound. Do not come back outside until it's over."

"Thanks, we'll remember. And once it's over, if Jack hasn't come home, we'll go out with you to look for him. You'll be able to cover three times the area that way," shouted Riss above the rising winds. She was always an animal lover and felt bad for Todd and Jack.

"Thanks guys. Stay safe!"

Riss and Lou went back into their house. Todd circled his steps before going back into his. He looked under the house, under the truck, and in the outdoor shower. But again, he found exactly what he expected to find, nothing. "Jack, where the hell are you?" he murmured to himself.

Back inside now, Todd closed the lone open hurricane shutter and decided to turn the generator off. "Might as well save gas," he thought. "No telling how long the power would be out. Could be days. Then again, could be weeks too." Besides, he didn't mind sitting in the dark for a while. He might even get some sleep that way.

Todd sprawled out on his couch. He loved his couch. It was eight feet long and brown leather. He had a hell of a time getting it up the stairs into the house. One of the drawbacks to living on stilts is that everything needed to be carried upstairs-- furniture, groceries, everything. Chuck was smart when he built his house on stilts. He installed an elevator that ran up and down the exterior of the house from ground level to the main living area. You couldn't fit a couch or any other piece of furniture in it, but at least you could bring all of your groceries up at one time.

As he lay on his couch, Todd looked back on the day, so much had transpired in less than 24 hours. He visited each of the job sites to make sure everything was secured. But there was no telling what it might look like now. He was more concerned about the Rodanthe project than the Hyatt. A lot more time would be lost on that job. Who knows when they might even be able to reach it again. He was sure that Highway 12 would be impassable right now. It was likely under literally tons of sand and water.

Todd's thoughts then drifted to the part of the day when he and Jack walked down to the sound to check things out. It was then and there that Todd remembered that he had forgotten to get gas. If Todd had gotten the gas when he wanted to on the way home, instead of forgetting, he had no doubt that Jack would be laying at his feet on the end of the couch. But he had forgotten, and now Jack was out braving the elements, maybe even dead, due to a stupid, stupid lapse of memory!

As Todd was replaying the events in his mind, he heard the wind howling and was praying the trees at the end of the street would be washed away by the sound waters which were no doubt rushing over their banks right now. With this thought, Todd drifted off to sleep. It had been twenty-four hours since he had woken up on Monday morning, and the stress of the days and evenings 'events had finally caught up to him.

Bam! Crack! Snap! "What the hell?" Todd yelled as he was suddenly startled awake. He was groggy and woke up to total darkness. It took a minute to get his bearings and figure out exactly where he was.

Slowly, as his mind came more into focus, Todd remembered he was at home, alone. Alone that is, except for Hurricane Izzy. She's turned out to be one of those summer house guests that have way overstayed their welcome. Todd decided to fire up the generator just long enough to make a pot of coffee. He could make it and then turn the generator back off to conserve the gas. After having two cups, he cracked open one of the hurricane shutters, the one that faced the street towards the ocean. That was where the dam of trees had collected earlier. He could still see sparking wires and what also looked to be a fire engine. The loud crash must have been a transformer that blew up. The brave men of the Kitty Hawk Fire Department were doing what they could to keep that fire from spreading to the houses on the street. With Izzy's winds, that seemed to be a herculean effort!

As for the dammed-up trees, Todd could tell there was standing water over there. How much water, he didn't know. It was still too dark to see well, but it was deep enough that it had some wave action. Not knowing exactly how long he had been asleep, it was hard to figure out how much longer this storm was going to last.

Chapter 19.

By the time Todd got to the bottom of the coffee pot, the winds seemed to have died down considerably. At least it didn't sound as loud as it had all night long. Todd opened one hurricane shutter and noticed that it did not seem so bad outside, so he opened all the others. Day break had come to the Outer Banks as Izzy made her departure for points inland. Apparently, she felt Elizabeth City was a lovely place to visit this time of year, so she made travel plans to visit that city as she climbed north and off of the Outer Banks.

Todd opened the door and carefully walked down the steps to the ground level. Thankfully, he parked the truck on the rise towards the rear of the underneath of the house because the flood waters from the sound had risen to the fourth step. The water level was at the middle of the tires, but nothing had gotten into the truck cab. Because he was on the rise of the street, the water wasn't nearly as deep at his house as it was at either end of the street. There was a current running down the street as he watched tree branches, garbage cans, lawn furniture, and kids' toys go floating by. He even noticed a dead squirrel or two. He hoped that someone else wasn't waking up this morning to see Jack's lifeless body drifting down their street.

There wouldn't be much clean- up done today. That wouldn't happen until the water receded significantly and the power crews came out to take care of the downed power lines. It would be a day of more rain and cabin fever. It was not likely that the power, T.V., or cell service would be restored at any point today either.

It would be a day spent with worry and boredom. Todd had no way to communicate with Kim to make sure she was ok. There was no way to check in either with Chuck or any of his crew. He also knew that his older brother, Bryant, and his friends back home in Cleveland would want to know that he was ok. They, just like he, would have to wait until communication could be restored to have those questions answered and fears laid to rest.

The rain had fallen in significant quantities for nearly a solid day now; there was at least 25 inches in total. It would be the kind of rain that Noah would have been glad to see, but no one else. The ground had become more than saturated. Tall pines were still in danger of toppling on fences, houses, and cars. It seemed you could just lean on a tree, and it would fall. The sound of the rain was the only thing that kept Todd company. He had no contact with anyone; he had no Jack by his side. Now he wished that he was at one of those hurricane parties, but those people were probably passed out from excess alcohol consumption at this point. When they did finally wake up, they would be in no condition to get any clean-up done.

Todd decided to crank up the generator again. He didn't want the refrigerator to warm up completely, although he was careful to not keep opening it, but soon he would need to. He'd have to grab something to eat and cook it on his indoor grill. On a whim, Todd decided to turn on Ocean 105. Maybe they were able to gain access to the station and start broadcasting under generator power. But no dice, they were still off the air. Next Todd decided to try one of the stations out of the Tidewater, Virginia area. He managed to tune one in to gather the latest news on Izzy.

The announcer, through the static, was relating the latest news from a coast guard fly over. The coast guard had put a Sikorsky MH-60 Jayhawk Helicopter in the air to fly the length of the Outer Banks from Hatteras Village, Izzy's landfall point, all the way to the North Carolina/Virginia border. The Jayhawk is a twin engine, medium range vehicle typically used for search and rescue missions and can fly a crew of four up to 300 miles. For this mission, however, it was used to report on the damage caused by Hurricane Izzy.

The coast guard crew was reporting that Hatteras Village was mostly underwater, and it appeared that 60-75% of the structures were leveled. The marina was completely destroyed. Some of the boats from the marina were picked up and tossed a full mile away. Further on up the road, there was more devastation, more buildings had been flattened and more roads had been washed away.

Highway 12 was buried under sand, debris, and a mix of both ocean and sound water. The three towns that make up the former settlement of Chicamacomico-- Salvo, Waves and Rodanthe-- were no longer three separate towns but rather a hodgepodge of debris, each one indiscernible from the other. Even the famous Chicamacomico LifeSaving Station that had endured along these storm-swept shores since 1874 suffered significant damage. Interestingly though, there seemed to be no rhyme or reason as to what had been destroyed. Some buildings were completely demolished while others seemed to have only sustained some minor roof damage. Flood waters, however, were all around.

Flying north along the coast, the coast guard came up on the Herbert C Bonner Bridge that spanned the Oregon Inlet. The bridge had buckled in the middle which was causing everyone on Hatteras Island to essentially be cut off from the northern towns of Nags Head, Kill Devil Hills, and Kitty Hawk.

This was the only way to travel by road, so ferry service would have to be established for residents to get back and forth for the next undetermined amount of time.

As the coast guard helicopter came further north, it veered to the west to fly over Wanchese and Manteo, the two towns on Roanoke Island. Wanchese had approximately two feet of water on the city streets but relatively little structural damage.

The boats and the buildings of the Wanchese Seafood Industrial Park seemed to come through the storm unscathed. Most of the commercial fisherman of the area worked out of this harbor and their livelihood was on the line.

Manteo fared about the same. There were lots of fallen trees and standing water in the city streets but relatively little building damage. The bell tower on top of the courthouse, that was ironically only replaced this past summer after being destroyed by another storm 80 years earlier, had miraculously survived Izzy. The bridge leading from the downtown area to Ice Plant Island and Festival Park had suffered some minor damage as did the Elizabeth II. The ship is a full size representative 16th Century sailing vessl that was designed and named after one of the seven ships used by Sir Walter Raleigh's fleet when he first brought colonists to Roanoke Island in 1587. The ship was commissioned to be part of the 400th anniversary celebration of the founding of Roanoke and America, the colony that famously became the "Lost Colony of Roanoke."

The Amphitheater located at Festival Park wasn't quite so lucky. The structure, which just this past summer hosted concerts by Bruce Hornsby, Todd Rungdren, and Don Henley, was shorn from its mountings and was leaning significantly towards the sound behind it.

Further up the island on the north end, the Lost Colony and Elizabethan Gardens, both part of the Historic Ft Raleigh, were sitting under about three feet of water, but no damage could be detected from the air. The Lost Colony Theater is where a play based on the accounts of Sir Walter Raleigh's attempts to establish a permanent settlement on Roanoke Island had been presented each night of the summer since 1937. It is located on the site of the original "Lost Colony," America's oldest unsolved mystery.

Heading back down the island to the south, the crew of the Coast Guard Jayhawk wanted to trace the path along the Manteo-Nags Head Causeway to ensure it was passable and not damaged in any way. What they witnessed was likened to what one would find on a battlefield. The causeway was littered with debris: trees, boats from the nearby Pirates Cove Marina, pieces of building structures that had flown off houses and businesses, battered street lights, and sparking electrical wires. It appeared, from the air anyway, that until the towns were able to bring in some heavy machinery to clear the mess, the causeway would remain impassable, essentially cutting Roanoke Island off from the beach and vice versa.

As the crew flew over Whalebone Junction and back north towards the northern beaches, they reported the standard flooding waters, though most did not affect any homes due to the homes being built on stilts. But certainly, some of the businesses had sustained some water damage as they sat on ground level.

As they flew over Kill Devil Hill, an irony was not lost on the crew. The Wright Brothers' Memorial, the site where Orville and Wilbur Wright flew the first "heavier than air" machine on December 17, 1903, stood proudly on her perch seeming to hardly even notice that a major hurricane had just passed it by.

However, the two wooden sheds that were based on historic photographs and recreated to mimic the world's first airplane hangar, the brother's living quarters, and the Visitor's Center were all sitting in flood waters.

Over Kitty Hawk, the crew was witnessing the same situation as everywhere else along the beach, flood waters and some wind damage to structures. All in all, the area had fared as well as could be expected. The one major report that the coast guard crew had was that all of the piers from Hatteras Village north were gone. In fact, in the ensuing days, it would be reported by NOAA -- the National Oceanic and Atmospheric Administration-- the folks tasked with "ensuring that ocean and coastal areas are safe, healthy and productive," that every pier within a distance of 170 miles of the coastline had been demolished.

As the coast guard crew made their way back to their home base in Elizabeth City for re-fueling, they did pass on some information, almost matter-of-factly. It was something that would significantly affect each and every Outer Banker.

All the cell towers had been completely destroyed during Izzy. There would be no cell phone communication any time soon. So, the Outer Banks was not only cut off, communication wise, from the outside world, they were also cut off from each other.

Those on Hatteras Island couldn't communicate with those on the beaches and vice versa. Those on Roanoke Island, even though they could see others from across the sound, were also cut off from those on the beach. Each Island was now in a world of its own, and that's exactly why the power company maintained stations for the crews to work out of in each of those areas.

Finally, the winds and rain were starting to diminish. In fact, very nice weather was starting to push through, as is often the case after such storms. They wreak havoc and then it is almost like they never existed, except for the damage they leave in their wake. However, it was still not safe enough to venture out just yet; a fact being reported by the Tidewater radio station: "Let the power company do their job first and make sure the downed power lines are no longer a hazard."

While Todd was listening in to the radio broadcast from Tidewater, Virginia, Kim was scurrying around trying to find something for Jack to eat. She found what was probably a five-year-old can of Dinty Moore's beef stew. It was in her pantry so long, she wasn't even sure how it got there. Though she would never eat it, she thought maybe Jack would enjoy it. Jack didn't seem to be a picky eater, in fact, he quite enjoyed it. Then again, he also enjoyed getting his water out of the toilet; a habit Kim wasn't especially fond of considering he also usually followed it up with a big, wet, sloppy kiss to whoever might be nearby. And that was usually Kim.

After Jack ate his beef stew, Kim realized that he hadn't been out to do his "business" since arriving late yesterday afternoon. Even though Jack never went anywhere with a leash, Kim thought it prudent that she not let him roam free with the flood waters and the sparking electrical wires all around.

She didn't have a leash, so she looked around frantically for something she could fashion one out of. She finally decided to use an extension cord as a make shift leash. There was no collar to tie it to because in Todd's words, "Jack didn't need a collar because he didn't belong to anyone."

"Yeah, wonder if he feels that now," Kim thought. So, Kim had to carefully tie the extension cord around Jack's neck-- snugly, but not too tight. After all, if it was too loose and he could just wiggle away, it would serve no purpose. They went out the back door as Jack was being led, for the first time in his life, with a leash around his neck. He didn't quite know what to make of it. They had to wade through the water to a rise towards the back of the yard. Kim just kept hoping that she wouldn't encounter a water snake along the way. Even though she grew up here with water snakes a plenty, she could never get over her squeamishness.

With Jack's business now complete, both Kim and Jack waded back to the house. She knew that Todd was probably very worried about her and the dog he didn't own, so she again picked up her cell phone to try and dial him. But it was dead; there was no cell service at all. With no power, she decided to turn off the phone to save its battery. If the phone died, she'd have to go to her Jeep and run that to recharge the battery. Thankfully, the Jeep stood tall enough to keep the flood waters out.

As she moved back over to the couch with Jack at her side, the image of Todd worrying through the storm about two things he didn't own, both she and Jack, crossed her mind. She thought it was funny, not a "ha ha" funny but an ironic funny.

As Kim sat on the couch with no power, no T.V., no cell phone, and no generator, she thought it was going to be a long, boring day. Unlike Todd, she wasn't able to listen to the station out of Tidewater, so she had no clue as to what happened throughout the night. Her world only extended to the plot of land that her house sat on. The houses on either side of her were rentals, and those folks evacuated prior to the storm, as anyone who wasn't a true Outer Banker would have done. Well, at least she had Jack to keep her company. Maybe the dog was smarter than anyone thought. Maybe that's exactly why he made the trek across the causeway to her back door before the storm.

Meanwhile, down the block at Chuck and Trish's, Chuck had his generator power and was listening to the same news report out of Tidewater that Todd was listening to. He felt bad for the people on Hatteras Island. It appeared those folks were going to have to rebuild their lives. He knew people who lived there; you don't live on secluded barrier islands your whole life without knowing the families that were also there for generations. They were family, friends, and customers, and they were going to have some daunting challenges in the days, weeks, and months ahead.

Chuck was thankful that he fared pretty well. Though not a religious man, he stopped and said a silent prayer of thanks. He was glad that Trish reminded him to bring the elevator car on the side of the house up to the main living area and not leave it down on the ground level like it usually was. If it had been left there, the elevator car would have been swamped with water right now. "Score one for the wife," he thought.

Chuck would sustain some property damage; the pool cover gave way and dumped all the sand and debris sitting on top of it into the once crystal-clear water. Now the cover frame, on which the motorized cover glided back and forth, would have to be replaced along with the cover itself. The pool and the filter would need one helluva cleaning.

All of that, Chuck could stomach. It was the store he was most worried about. As he looked down the street through the other yards in the neighborhood towards Highway 64, he could see standing water. He just didn't know how far it extended. If it made it all the way to the door step of the Roanoke Island Outfitters Group, would it be deep enough to cause any damage? He didn't know. There was nothing to do but wait. He had to wait until given the all clear that it would be safe enough to go out to survey the damage. Hopefully, that piece of news would come later today.

As the new day was dawning and the winds and rain all but completely stopped, Chuck opened up the hurricane shutters to let in the fresh air. It always smelled cleaner after a big storm, as if everything was washed anew again. With the generator power on, Trish made some coffee, eggs, and sausage. "Might as well have a good breakfast," she said to Chuck, "while we're just sitting around waiting."

Once breakfast was finished and the generator was back off, Chuck tried to complete some paperwork that needed to be finished: payroll, inventory balancing sheets, and things like that. But he was not able to concentrate on those mundane tasks.

His mind was wandering on his little sis, Kim, and how she made it through the storm. Even though she was just down the street, she was just far enough out of sight for him to not know what it was like for her there. Judging by what he could see from the surrounding neighborhood, he thought she was probably ok, but you just never know about a rogue tree falling. She did have that tall pine just outside the front door.

He also wondered about Todd. He wondered how things were going for him on the beach. The reports from the coast guard crew seemed promising, but again, you never know about any individual house. Chuck had a whole lot of questions but very few answers. He knew he wouldn't be getting those answers anytime soon with the report that cell towers were down and out of service for who knows how long. It was more than just the storm damage that Chuck was worried about with Todd. He was also concerned about Hurricane Kim. Even though she was his sister, Chuck knew the damage she could do to Todd. He'd seen it before, first hand.

The one other thing he dreaded was that while the people who lived there were trying to get things back in order, Chuck knew that the hurricane curiosity seekers would be flooding (pardon the pun) back in once the county opened up the roads again. Nothing interferes with clean-up progress more than a bunch of damn curiosity hounds.

Chapter 20.

It had been a long day on the Outer Banks as the sun set over
the mainland. It gets dark on the Outer Banks sooner than
almost everywhere else since it's the furthest point east on the
continental United States.

As this sun set, it brought an end to a day that had two
spectrums: one that was extremely busy, and one that was
long and boring. The busy ones were the power people who
did their best to neutralize all the downed electrical lines.
They were expecting back-up help from other power
companies further inland and to the north and south, but they
hadn't arrived yet. It looked like, for them, it was going to be
an equally long night trying to restore at least some of the
power.

Hatteras Island was not going to get power anytime soon, that
much was a given. It really wouldn't matter much anyway
with so many of the houses and businesses already destroyed.
The infrastructure had been completely undermined there.
The power people could start on the northern beaches, towns
like South Nags Head, Nags Head, Kill Devil Hills, Kitty
Hawk, Southern Shores, Duck and Corolla. The crew on the
island would be doing what they could to get power restored
to both Wanchese and Manteo. The goal, according to the
news reports from the Tidewater radio station, was to get at
least 10% power restored by daybreak tomorrow.

The crew at the Roanoke Island Fire Department was loading
up their big truck with some supplies: bottles of water,
batteries, various toiletries, and a crew that ordinarily didn't
ride on the trucks.

The staff at Ocean 105 was eager to get back to their studios to start supplying the residents of the Outer Banks with the news that they all sought. They weren't sure yet that they could get into the station that was carved out of the swamp. If they did, what were they going to find---standing water, snakes? There were plenty of those in the neighborhood, and if they did find the studios habitable, would they be able to get that World War II surplus generator cranked up and running again? They would know in the next half hour or so. The coast guard crew had been in contact with the police and fire on the Outer Banks, and from the air, they thought Highway 64 leading from the north end of the island to the south end would be passable by fire truck. They just couldn't be 100% positive. The fire chief thought it was important to try, so off they went.

Immediately, as they turned the truck onto Highway 64, they were faced with an obstacle. A rather large pine tree had fallen across the road. Their first inclination was to go around it, but with the amount of rain that area had endured the last few days, it didn't seem prudent to get any part of the wheels near the water-logged grass. Instead, the chief had two of his guys jump out. The water was ankle deep where they were. They grabbed the gas-powered Stihl chain saws and made short work of the tree, tossing the limbs off to the side of the road. "It's gonna be a longer ride than we originally thought," the chief said to the radio station staff.

The truck moved in a southerly direction and reached the entrance to Manteo High School. Looking off to his left, the chief, whose son is the stud quarterback for the team while he is the public-address announcer, noticed immediately that the press box overlooking the football stadium was shorn off. There was supposed to have been a home game this Friday night against the Topsail Beach Pirates.

"Unlikely that's going to happen now." The chief silently thanked Izzy for the damaged press box. "Damn press box needed to be renovated anyway," he said. "Needed to be for years."

The fire engine continued its slow, methodical journey towards the radio station. They left the other truck at the station to respond to any emergencies should there be any. Hurricanes and their low-pressure systems are notorious for bringing pregnant women into premature labor. There seems to be one every storm.

As far as the crew on the move, they got as far south as the Christmas Shop. The shop had new owners now as the original owner just sold it and retired a few months ago. What timing he had on that decision! The big Christmas Shop sign that tourists looked for when coming over to the island was splintered, and bits and pieces of wood were strewn across the parking lot. The storm sewer was clogged with debris making the draining of the standing water a very slow process. The building appeared ok, at least from the outside. It would need a good deal of landscape clean- up, however, as trees had been uprooted all throughout the property.

Off to the right, the 7-11, where the fire crew would often go for snacks during their shift and for a six pack on their way home, seemed to not even know of anyone or anything named Izzy. For them, nothing at all was out of place. The store had no damage that could be seen from the outside. The roof was intact-- there was no broken glass, no flood waters up to the door, and even the trees that separate the store from their neighbors stood upright and proud. In fact, the only thing that seemed out of place was that it was closed.

Just a block down the road, the Hardee's wasn't quite so lucky. The store front was caved from the outside in. There were trees lying on top of the building and the flood waters were lapping at its doors. There was no doubt that the water had breached the inside. It almost looked like a total tear down and rebuild was going to be necessary.

In what usually takes approximately three minutes to drive took closer to 15 tonight. The fire engine and the two crews got to the junction on the island where, if you headed east over the causeway, you'd end up on the beach. If you took the bridge to the west, you would be on the mainland in Stumpy Point and Mashoes. Having heard the damage reports on the causeway and knowing that it was completely blocked, the fire chief focused his gaze to the east. It was getting darker with each passing moment, and it was really hard to see what it actually looked like, although he did see a rather odd sight. There were at least a dozen boats that were on the roadway and what looked like another handful that were in various stages of being swamped. "Total mess," he thought.

As they pushed further south through the southern part of the island towards the radio station, the terrain changed dramatically. There were very few buildings here, mostly just swamp land. So other than the water being a bit higher, there was nothing really out of the ordinary. Swamps have a way of adapting to Mother Nature and neither seems to bother the other very often. The only difference tonight were the speed bumps they felt every few feet. The speed bumps on Highway 64 were actually water moccasins that were crossing the road from one side of the swamp to the other. They were big enough, apparently, to make it feel like you were driving over a speed bump. Though wildlife is an important part of the Outer Banks, this is one animal that the residents could do with less of.

It was just a couple more miles up the winding road to Ocean 105. The running joke amongst the locals was that the radio station would be better named Swampy 105 due to its location.

Standing water on the road hadn't really been an issue. At its deepest along the way, it only came half-way up the tires of the truck. That was a good sign as it meant the waters were now retreating back into the sound. It did make it hard for keeping on the road, however, and without being able to see the actual street, the engine driver missed a curve a couple of times and had to back onto the road and try again. That significantly impeded their progress. Unlike the cell towers, the radio tower could be seen standing tall and proud in the distance. The tallest structure on the entire island looked no worse for wear. Now, hopefully, the building looked more like the 7-11 and not the Hardee's. In a few more minutes, they would know.

As they pulled into the station parking lot, right away they noticed that the water was still about two feet deep. Thankfully, the station, having been built off the ground by four or five feet, was high and dry. The trailer out front that served as an office had sustained a significant amount of damage from the water when they were all rescued from Izzy, but it was once again sitting above the swamp.

The general manager realized that in their haste to get out the previous night, no one had locked the front door. "Oh well," he thought. "It's not like anyone was out and about last night or today. Plus, the people who live around here are all friends and neighbors. It wasn't like being in New York City, or some other large city, when a natural disaster hits and the area is plagued by looters. No, that wasn't a news story that would hit the airwaves down here."

As both crews walked into the hexagon shaped building that housed the on-air studio-- the production studio and the news and program directors' offices-- the carpet squished under their feet. There was no doubt that water had gained access at some point. How much, they didn't know. Everything else still seemed to be in place: the autographed poster of World Champion surfer Ken Bradshaw still hung on the wall, a remembrance of when he came to the Outer Banks to promote his new line of surfboards at one of the local surf shops. The picture of former morning guy, Bryant Richards, and the news director standing on the concession stand at Lake Matamuskeet High School broadcasting the football game while being pelted by rocks was still in its place just outside the on-air studio as well.

The radio station engineer and the station general manager went out to the generator in the rear of the building. They were very careful to not upset any water moccasins that might be lingering. They started the ancient machine, and she came to life! Step one was successful! Well, step two anyway. Step one was just getting there. Next, the two men flipped the switch that threw the generator power over to the studio building. The flicks flickered and came on very dimly. The rest of the crews went around cutting off as many lights as they could to conserve what little power they had. Now step three was complete, and it was time to go on to step four.

The engineer and general manager went into the transmitter room, which had to be turned on in stages. First, they would have to throw a switch to allow everything to warm up. Then they would need to throw a second switch to put them live on the air.

They held their collective breaths as the engineer threw the first switch and nothing happened. That took the air out of everyone's sails.

If they couldn't get the transmitter up, then this entire trip would have been for naught, not to mention that those people with power or generator power were counting on them to provide the latest news on the storm. At the moment, everyone was cut off from everyone else. If Ocean 105 were able to get back on the air, at least everyone would know how their friends and neighbors were doing. It's a strange feeling when you live in an area where everyone knows everyone else's business because you're that close knit. Yet no one knew how anyone else was doing now because there was no power.

The engineer tried again, but there was still nothing. The third attempt brought the same result. The engineer then opened the front of the transmitter. He took a quick look at the wires and switches inside and discovered a circuit breaker that had been tripped, so he flipped that switch and closed up the front of the transmitter. He tried the first switch again, and this time, there was nothing again! The engineer stepped back for a moment to survey the situation. He traced back in his mind all the steps. "The generator is working because they have lights in the studio, so that's not it." He pondered what else it could be.

Often times the thing that seems the most difficult can be solved by the simplest solution. The overnight DJ, the guy with the least amount of experience in radio, was afraid to speak up. He knew everyone just thought he was wet behind the ears, but he mustered the courage to speak.

"Um, the switch was flipped to turn the generator power to the studio. Did anyone flip the switch to turn it on in the transmitter room?" The engineer and general manager looked at each other and fell down laughing.

"Son-of-a-bitch! Out of the mouths of babes," the engineer screamed. They went back into the room, turned on the switch to get power to it, waited a second, and again held their breath as they flipped the first transmitter switch. It was glowing green. "It's on!" They now had to wait for about a minute before throwing the second switch because they had to allow the transmitter time to warm up.

That minute felt like hours. The engineer kept track of the time on his watch. It was time now to throw the second switch and hopefully put Ocean 105 on the air for everyone on Roanoke Island and the beaches to hear. The engineer reached over to the second switch. He flipped it, and the station that broadcasts a prayer for the fishermen each morning as they go out to the gulf stream to earn a living and support their families was back live on the air! How many, if any, were listening at that moment was inconsequential. They were there to supply news and information on the cleanup of the storm to whomever might be out there listening.

Todd sat in the ever-encroaching darkness, unaware, yet, that his brother's old radio station was back on the air. It was the second night now without Jack. With any luck, the morning light would bring more of the cleanup as crews worked through the night. If the street was cleared of the tree dam, then Todd planned on taking the truck out to look for Jack. If the trees still lay in the street, then Todd planned on walking the mile over to his shop to grab a chainsaw and start the clearing himself.

He then decided, before it got too dark to see, to throw a swordfish steak on the grill. He didn't know how much longer the area might be without power, so he thought it would be best to start using up things in the refrigerator before they went bad.

He had been starting and stopping the generator frequently throughout the day and night to keep a cool enough temperature for the food.

Todd stepped outside onto the deck to light the grill. Lou and Riss were doing the same thing across the street. Todd shouted "Hello", and they replied back:

"We've been thinking about you all day. Any sign of Jack yet?"

"No," Todd responded. "If they don't clear the trees at the bottom of the street tonight, then I'm going to do it myself so I can go out to look for him."

Lou yelled out, "Either way, let me know. God knows I've got plenty of work to do around here, but if you need help clearing the trees, I'll give you a hand. It will go faster that way."

"What about your store?" Todd asked. "Don't you need to open it? People are going to need supplies."

"No power, so not open for business," Lou yelled back. "Besides, my shelves are pretty much bare from when people bought their supplies before Izzy. Until I can get a truck in here, there's not much to sell right now."

"Good point."

"I'll help with the tree clearing and then start on my yard and house. Riss will go out with you to look for Jack once we can get your truck off the street."

"Deal," Todd said as he decided the young kids might make for great neighbors after all. Prior to the storm, they had been courteous to one another but had never really engaged in any conversation. "I tell you what. After this is all over, we'll go down to the Happy Dolphin for fish tacos. My treat."

"You don't have to do that Todd," Riss responded. "But we've been hearing about those world famous fish tacos since moving here and haven't taken the time to try them. Now we have a reason. Thanks!"

With that, Todd's swordfish steak was done. He bid the couple a good evening and went back inside. Normally he'd eat outside on the deck, but he had dragged all the outside furniture in ahead of the storm. After finishing his swordfish and the baked potato he threw into the microwave, Todd dragged all the furniture back outside and laid on the outside couch a long while. It was a pretty evening and the stars were starting to come out. "You couldn't see stars like this in his hometown of Cleveland, or any other big city," he thought.

Kim, still one of the several hundred people without power on the island, decided that she was going to walk down the street to her big brother Chuck's house. The waters had mostly retreated, and all of the downed power lines had been attended to. She had been cooped up in that house way too long. Being the free spirit that she was, it was all she could bear to be held prisoner in one spot by a storm named Izzy.

Not wanting to take a chance on Jack darting away, she grabbed the extension cord that she had been using to take Jack out to the yard. She tied it, once again around his neck, and walked down the block. "Lots of downed trees," she thought to herself as she made her way north.

Storm sewers blocked with debris kept the water puddled up in the streets and in some yards. Overall, it appeared that her part of Roanoke Island wasn't nearly as bad as it could have been.

Kim got to Chuck's house. As she walked under the house to go to the back door, she saw that the in-ground pool in the back yard was in a world of hurt. The pool cover had caved in as the weight of the sand and debris was just too much for it to hold. It was going to require a lot of work to be made right again. Kim thought back to earlier in the summer when she, Chuck, Trish, and Todd had a cookout at the pool together. Chuck had this big inflatable killer whale toy that he had for the neighborhood kids when they came by to swim. Todd had had a few too many OBX Blondes, the beer brewed locally down the street at the Manteo Brewing Company, and climbed up on the toy killer whale. After about five attempts of sliding off, Todd found his balance and yelled to the other three, "Look at me. I'm a killer whale tamer." As he floated on the toy around the pool, he yelled out for all to hear. "I'm going to get business cards that read: Todd Richards, Killer Whale tamer!" That was all Kim could take. She swam underneath Todd and the Killer Whale and dumped him off of it.

"There," she said. "Now the whale may swim free again! Free Willy! Free Willy!" She screamed.

The thought of that night made her smile and a warm, fuzzy feeling came over her. It was at that exact moment that she knew that she and Todd were kindred spirits. After all this silly Izzy business was over, she had to have a conversation with him to make this work.

Climbing the back stairs to the house, Kim walked in the door onto the outside patio and then into the house in the dining room. Since they were family, they never knocked before entering one another's homes.

The sudden commotion of a dog and a person walking into the dining room startled Trish.

"Oh," Trish yelled out. "I didn't expect anyone."

"Sorry," replied Kim. "I just couldn't stay locked up in that house alone any longer. The walls were closing in on me."

"I get that," Trish said. "Chuck was the same way. Must run in the family."

"Where is my big brother?"

"He also couldn't sit around here anymore. He decided to walk down to the store now that it's safe. But without power, he's not going to be able to see much."

"No, probably not, but he'll at least be able to assess whether there was much damage or not."

"Yeah," Trish said. "You know, his whole life is wrapped up in that store. Just as he was starting to ease off and spend more time with me at home, I'm afraid he'll be back there more than full time again until things are back on their feet."

"Probably so. But look at the positive side. Once it is, he can slack off again. If I know anything about my big brother, deep, down inside, he doesn't want to work that hard. At least not anymore."

"Sigh. You're right Kim. How about we open a bottle of wine and wait for him to get back? You pick out a bottle, and I'll wrestle up some food for this mange mutt."

With that, Kim walked over to the wine rack and picked out a bottle of French Beaujolais. As she did, she remarked to Trish, "Seems like you guys are keeping up with that wine of the month Christmas present I got you last year. Not a whole lot left sitting here."

Trish poured some dog food into a bowl for Jack. "Well, you know, being married to your brother isn't easy. I have to have something to settle my nerves."

With that, they both laughed. When the bottle was 3/4 of the way gone, Chuck came bounding in the door. He was surprised to see his little sister, Kim, and even more surprised to see Jack.

"How in the world do you have Jack?" He asked.

"Well, to tell the truth, I'm not sure," Kim replied. "As Izzy was just about to crank up, I heard a bit of a ruckus at the back door. I went to investigate it, and boom, Jack came crashing through the door. Scared the bejesus out of me!"

"Does Todd know he's here?"

"No. At least I don't think so. I got on the phone to tell him, but just as I was about to, the cell service went down."

"Wow! I'm sure that boy is sick with worry. Of course, he'll never admit that. But I got to tell you, you had me worried too. After checking the store, I walked down to your house to check in on you. The back door was unlocked and the house was empty. I didn't know where you were. I was hoping maybe Kallie's, but I didn't know for sure."

"Aww, big brother cares about me. That's sweet."

"Don't let it go to your head, lil sis. I was worried about our ancestral home."

"Yeah, whatever. How's the Outfitter's store?" Kim asked.

"I don't think too badly, though it's tough to know in the dark. No structural damage of any sort, and I don't think any water got in. I think we got lucky this time."

"Yeah, not like last time when it took us three months to open back up," Trish chimed in. "And that was just the result of a Nor'easter." With that, Trish poured the remainder of the wine equally into both her and Kim's glasses.

Chuck walked over to the wine rack, pulled out another bottle for the girls, this time a Shiraz, and grabbed a beer for himself. "Who's hungry?" Chuck yelled out.

"I can eat a horse," Kim replied back.

"Yeah, me too," Trish said.

With that, Chuck grabbed some steaks out of the refrigerator. "Hmmm, got four here, and one will go bad if we don't use it. Kim, why don't you run out to Kallie's and see if she'd like to eat with us while I start the grill?"

"Roger that big bro." Kim took Jack, attached to that ridiculous extension cord, with her and walked downtown to Kallie's apartment above the book store. It seemed a little bit eerie as she walked through the deserted streets. The trees were in a big heap everywhere, and the street lights were still out.

"Well, at least I got you big fella." She stooped down to pet Jack. "Yeah, right. If anything happens, I already know that it's gonna be me protecting you, you mange ole mutt."

Kim climbed the stairs to the apartment and knocked on Kallie's door. There was no answer at first as Kallie was sleeping on the couch. With the windows boarded shut, it was hard to tell when it was day and when it was night. Kallie, thinking it was like 11a.m. and not about 7 p.m., was already asleep. She groggily got up and accepted the dinner invitation with Kim and her family.

As they were chowing down on the steaks, asparagus, and sweet potato biscuits, (yes, they're not just for breakfast), Kallie was talking excitedly about the surf that would be the result of Izzy. "Sure, we can't get to the point down on Hatteras Island, but once the causeway is clear, we can surf the break that is sure to be where the Avalon Pier once stood."

"You go ahead Kallie. My big brother is too old and feeble to be getting the store back into shipshape on his own. I reckon he'll be needing my help."

Chuck stared at his little sister. "You mean you're going to pass up the surf of the year to help me? You feeling alright?"

"Chuck, leave her alone," Trish said. "Kim that is so wonderful of you to help."

"I just do what I can, with what little I got," Kim chuckled.

"What?" All three asked in unison.

"Oh, nothing. Just something Todd says all the time." Kim smiled softly to herself as she said it.

Trish, who noticed the smile, made a mental note. "I'll be having a private little talk with sister-in-law soon," she thought.

With dinner over, Chuck and Trish walked the girls back to their homes and then took a quick walk to the Manteo Dock. The waters of Shallowbag Bay were so peaceful. It hardly seemed like they could have been raging just 24 hours ago.

Chapter 21.

Todd woke with a sudden shudder. He had no idea what time it was. He was still on the outdoor couch. "The stars were still out, so it must still be very early morning," he thought. There was no sign of the sun rising over the ocean just yet. He laid there not knowing that Kim, Jack, Chuck, and Trish were ok over in Manteo. It felt like he had been out of touch with the people that meant so much to him more than just the 36 hours that it had been. He tried the internet; he thought if he could get an email to them, then he would know if everything was ok or not. But the internet was also still down. He felt more alone right now than he had felt in a long time.

With each passing day, hour, minute, and second, it seemed less and less likely that Jack could have made it through the storm. He would have made his way back home by now; Todd was sure of it. The only hope Todd had left was that at the beginning of the storm someone saw Jack out wandering and brought him into their home. Maybe they'd decided to keep him in the process. How could they know that someone would be worried about a dog that was out wandering without a dog tag or a collar?

Todd stumbled off the couch. He went to go fix a pot of coffee and take a shower. The outside shower was still packed with debris, so Todd took one inside. It was the first time he'd done that in about a year. "One way to keep the bathtub clean," he would joke to Kim, "is to not use it."

While in the shower, just for the hell of it, he tried to turn on Ocean 105, on the radio that sat on the bathroom counter;

he had flipped to generator power to have lights for the shower and power for the coffee pot. He was pleasantly surprised that they were back on the air. The signal was fairly weak, indicating that they were on generator power, but they were on the air! That had to mean that Roanoke Island wasn't decimated like Hatteras Island was. He felt like he could rest a bit easier now, at least as far as Kim, Chuck, and Trish were concerned.

Nothing new was being reported on Ocean 105 that he hadn't already heard on the Tidewater, Virginia station last night. It made sense, though, since the Coast Guard crew wouldn't have been able to assess much more of the damage with the passing of the night. He was hoping that when daybreak came they'd be back on the air reporting again.

After drying off quickly from his very cold shower, there was still no hot water in the house, Todd grabbed his first cup of coffee and decided to crack a couple eggs into a frying pan. He also threw a couple pieces of rye bread into the toaster. Todd gobbled up his breakfast just as the morning light started to peak across the Atlantic Ocean to the east.

Todd switched the generator back off and opened up all of the windows and doors to air the place out. The house had been shut up for too long, and there was nothing like a gentle ocean breeze wafting through to make things feel new and fresh again. He threw on some work pants, a t-shirt, and a pair of boots, and made his way down to the dam that Mother Nature, with the help of a storm called Izzy, created. The trees were still there, as he knew they would be. He figured the city would be responding to much more significant damages than just a bunch of fallen trees and branches across a side street.

He walked back to his house to grab his keys to the shop. He was going to grab either a chain saw, or, if the path was clear enough for the mile between the shop and the house, one of the front-end loaders to clear the dam. As he left the house to walk to the shop, he heard Lou call out across the street.

"Hey Todd. Are the trees still blocking the street?"

"Yeah," Todd yelled back. "I'm on my way to the shop now to grab whatever I can to clear it so we can all get out."

"Well, hold up five minutes," Lou yelled back. "Let me get some pants and boots on, and I'll help you."

Todd took the opportunity to drain the last cup of coffee from his pot while waiting. A few minutes later, Lou was at his door and ready to go.

On the walk over, Todd explained to Lou that he'd rather get the front-end loader and just push everything to the side. But that would depend on the roads. If they were blocked and he couldn't drive the equipment to the house, then he'd grab a couple of chainsaws and do it the hard way.
On the walk to the shop, Todd found out that while the young couple moved here from Atlanta, they were originally from Cleveland, born and raised there. And as it turned out, they had lived in Mayfield Heights. Todd was from South Euclid, and the two towns were no more than five miles apart, maybe even less.

But Lou and Riss were significantly younger. In fact, Todd could be their father, so they had no common friends back on the Northcoast.

Lou and Riss met while in grade school. They stayed together through high school, went through college at The Ohio State University, and then they moved to Atlanta after getting married, where Riss took an accounting job for CNN. They thought it would be a great start for their young lives, but the pull of wanting to do something for themselves, rather than working for a very large corporation where you are treated more like a number than a person, was too great to ignore. So, two years later, they decided to risk it all and open the hardware store on the Outer Banks. Lou knew the "nuts and bolts" of the business. That pun always made Riss groan, though Lou thought it was brilliant.

Riss knew the bookkeeping part, so they put everything on the line and gave it a go. Both of their families had vacationed here since before they were born, so they felt a bond with these barrier islands. The place had been home since May. Todd could relate to their story. His family had vacationed here too. They'd been coming since the 1970's, well before Lou and Riss were even born. Though it was his brother Bryant who made the first move here, it was Todd who had made the place home for thirty years now. Again, this was before Lou and Riss were even born.

As they walked along, Todd decided that they would never get the front-end loader through. There were too many downed trees along the way, and he didn't dare drive around them onto the very saturated grass as it would no doubt just sink into it. No, they would have to do it the hard way, pretty much as Todd figured it would be.

Once arriving at the shop, Todd felt lucky that he had moved everything to the second level. There was significant evidence that the water had gained entry into the building.

Although it had drained back out again, it had been there at some point. There were plenty of downed limbs and scattered debris in the small parking lot too. It would take some time to clean up this mess.

Todd and Lou grabbed a couple of Stihl 21-inch chain saws and a backpack leaf blower to help clear the debris from the street. They closed the shop back up and started walking the mile back home. Lou told Todd to not worry about the saw blades since Todd would be doing a service for the community by clearing the street for everyone. Lou said he would sharpen the blades, once they were done, at no charge down at the hardware store.

Back at the house, they set about cutting up the tress and limbs to open up the street again, and more of the neighbors came out to lend a hand. The lesbian couple cleared the branches once they were made small enough by Todd and Lou's efforts. The older couple, who retired here from Virginia, provided sweet tea for those that were working, and the kids in the neighborhood came out looking to play with Jack. Todd had to explain to them that Jack had wondered off before the storm hit, and he didn't know where he was.

"Is Jack ok, Mr. Todd?" One of the eight-year-old little girls asked.

"I'm sure he is honey. Jack is a smart dog; he knows how to stay safe."

"Then why hasn't he come back home yet, Mr. Todd?"

Todd didn't have an answer for that, so he just told the little girl that he would be home soon. But first, Jack was just making sure that everyone else was safe. Todd lied. He didn't really think he was ever going to see that dog again.

It took the rest of the morning to clear up the trees in the street. Afterwards, the older couple offered to hire Todd and Lou to clean up their yard. They knew Todd owned his own landscape company, and for whatever reason, they thought Lou worked for him. Todd and Lou agreed to do the cleanup but wouldn't accept any pay. "This is a time when community comes together to help each other out, not gouging them for monetary gain," Todd said. Lou agreed as did the lesbian couple. In fact, everyone pitched in to clear out the yard for the older couple. From there they went up the street, one house at a time. Next was the lesbian couple's yard, followed by Lou, and then finally Todd's yard. Each person pitched in to help out one another. Even Riss came out to do some manual labor, even though it was quite evident that she wasn't accustomed to it.

By the time the yards were all cleaned up, the sun was starting to set on Kitty Hawk. Yet there was still no sign of power being restored to the area as the street lights remained unlit, as they had the previous two nights.

The older couple had a refrigerator full of hamburgers and hot dogs that they were going to use with their kids and grandkids before the storm, but Izzy had put a significant dent into those plans. So instead, they suggested that the street have an impromptu block party to celebrate that they were all still in good health and really no worse for the wear.

Everyone had worked up a healthy appetite doing yard clean up, so they all readily agreed. The lesbian couple had a case of beer that they brought over, and Lou and Riss had a salad that they were able to throw together. Todd apologized for being a bachelor and not having much to offer for the party. Everyone assured him that he needn't worry since it was his chainsaws and leaf blower that allowed them to get their yards in reasonable shape.

At first Todd was reluctant to stay and be a part of the celebration because it didn't feel right. He was finally about to blow off some steam, but he had no clue if either Jack or Kim were safe and sound. He felt like he needed to sit home and worry about their safety until he was able to bring this to some sort of closure.

Then suddenly, much like when Kim had her "aha moment" at Chuck and Trish's pool earlier the night before, Todd had his. At that moment, he realized that for someone who was just supposed to be his friend and not a love interest, he cared way too much about Kim's safety. He realized that if she was safe from this storm, he was going to do whatever it took to make this thing work between them. And with that thought, he smiled to himself, bit into a hamburger, cracked open a beer, and tried to enjoy himself as best he could.

The block party went on into the night, lit only by the fire in the fire pit of the older couple's backyard. Everyone was hoping for power the next day, or at least cell or internet service. They were hoping for anything that would allow them to communicate with the outside world, to let friends and family know that they were alright and that they were stronger than Hurricane Izzy. They wanted to let them know that as a community it was going to take more than 115 MPH winds to beat them. As of right now, it was only this group of seven people who knew that the others were safe from the storm. No one back in Virginia, Ohio, or hell, even on Roanoke Island knew it.

As far as anyone could guess, it was about 1 am when the party finally broke up; it was a long day. It was also a productive day. Everyone decided it was time to go home and get some sleep. As they each split up and went their separate ways home, Riss asked Todd if he was going to go look for Jack in the morning.

"Yes, I'm going to attempt to," he said.

"Good. Please stop by our house before you leave. Lou and I want to help."

"Lou does too? I thought you were the animal lover of the family."

"Oh, I am," Riss said. "But Lou knows how much Jack means to you, and he wants to help too."

"More like you told him to help," Todd replied.

"Yeah, that might have been it too," Riss laughed.

Todd promised he would stop by before leaving. With that, everyone was tucked safely into their homes for the evening. Then Todd started wondering about his crew. He told them to stay home the one day and get their homes in order, but he hadn't left any further instructions after that; he had no way to reach them. He knew the Rodanthe House crew wouldn't be able to get to their job site anyway, but he wondered if the Hyatt crew would try to make it to work in the morning. Todd figured that before he started looking for Jack, he had better drive to the homes of the three guys from the Hyatt crew who lived on the beach before they left for work. He needed to let them know that until power and cell service returned, they should remain home with their families. He would also tell them not to worry about having this time off without pay; he would figure out a way to make sure they could still make their financial obligations.

Todd pulled out his wind-up alarm clock that he kept for those occasions where there wasn't any power.
After all, the weather plays havoc with such things when you're living in a coastal community.

Todd set the alarm for 5:30 a.m. so he could make it out to the guys' houses from the Hyatt crew before they left for work.

Chapter 22.

Five thirty comes awfully early in the morning when you don't hit the pillow until just before 2 am. Todd stumbled out of bed and quickly got ready to leave for his crews' houses; it's easier to get ready when you've slept in your clothes all night.

Todd started the truck. Luckily, it had been sitting above the water line. He had no idea how close he'd be able to get to each guy's house. He already had figured out that if their streets were anything like his, then he probably was going to have to do some walking. Thankfully, he left as early as he did because that's exactly what happened. Todd was able to get the truck down the bypass to Kill Devil Hills without much problem, but each side street was impassible. He thought that each guy would need to make his own decision about whether to stay home, but he decided to pay each one a visit anyway.

He felt sick when he got to the first house. This house suffered significant damage. It was built on stilts, so the water didn't get in, but the winds certainly did a number on it. Part of the roof was blown off and a tree fell into a corner of the other side. His guy Zach was awake, and when Todd found him, he was just waiting for the sun to come up so he could do what he could to continue working on the repairs. Todd assured him that he could take as much time as he needed. They weren't going to work today, and it was likely that they wouldn't be working for the next few days. Todd also promised that he'd be back later in the day to help him with any necessary work that needed to be done. Zach thanked him and thought to himself, "That's why it's such a pleasure working for this guy. He could be making a fortune right now with all the clean-up that needs to be done on the beach, but he's more concerned about his crew and their families."

Todd made his way to the second and the third guys' houses. They were also both up and wondered if they should be making their way up to the Duck-Corolla line to start the clean-up of the Hyatt project. Todd assured them that with Izzy's damage, he was sure that the owners would have to push back their opening anyway. "Don't risk life and limb to get up there. There is no power anyway. All the interior work crews wouldn't be working and besides, the ground was too saturated at this point." He did, however, let them know about Zach's predicament and mentioned that if they were up to doing some work, they could join him later in giving Zach a hand. Both guys agreed, as Todd knew they would. It was a good group of guys he had working for him. He knew they would all have each other's backs.

That little errand took a little longer than he thought it would. Driving down the bypass was easier than he thought, but the time spent walking down each street to each individual house really slowed him up. It was close to 9am by the time Todd made it back home again.

As he pulled in the driveway, Riss came rushing over. "I thought you were going to stop by before leaving to go look for Jack this morning."

"I didn't go looking," Todd explained. "I had to go make contact with my crew to let them know not to try and report for work today. Wasn't so easy considering there's no cell service and I had to log about three miles on foot in total to get down each of their streets. The walk back to the Villa's Condo development took extra-long. The road is so long and curved. Let me just grab a quick shower. We did all that work yesterday, and I've not had a chance to get cleaned up just yet."

It was a quick shower too as the water was just as cold as it had been the day before.

When Todd finished up, he threw on his cargo shorts and a t-shirt, and he found Riss and Lou already outside ready to go. Todd threw an old blanket in the bed of the truck just in case Jack was all muddy and wet. The three climbed into the cab of Todd's truck with Riss in the middle. "You kids sure you want to give up a good part of your day when it's likely that we won't find him?"

"You hush up Todd," Riss snapped back. "You have to go into this with a positive attitude. It won't do us or Jack any good if you're not positive."

"Good point," Todd replied. It would have been the exact same thing Kim would've said to him if she were here, he thought.

"Where should we start?" Lou asked.

"Well, I was getting gas at the Sunoco just past the Outer Banks Mall when Jack went missing. I thought we could park the truck there and start looking. We could cover the west side of the bypass first, then the east, and then move down the block searching in that pattern."

"Sounds like a plan," Riss added.

As they drove south down the bypass, they could see across the waters of the sound to Roanoke Island. Since all communications were still down, it might as well have been Australia. The causeway was still closed, and judging by what they were saying on Ocean 105, it wasn't expected to be open in the immediate future.

There was also some structural damage to the bridge that needed to be checked out. Boats weren't even a viable choice right now because there weren't many that escaped the storm unscathed. They had either been blown completely out of the water and were still stacked up on the causeway, or they were in various stages of swamping. Not to mention, it would be too dangerous to take to the waters of the sound right now. There was so much debris floating on top, and even more importantly to a boater, debris was just beneath the surface where it couldn't be seen, sure suicide for boats and boaters.

The trip down the bypass took no time at all. All the traffic lights were still out, but luckily, there wasn't much traffic either. Most of the side streets were clogged by debris from the storm and were still cut off from the bypass, keeping most people home and off the streets. There was plenty of activity though on each street as homeowners were out doing what they could do to clean up. One of the problems, however, was that a lot of the housing stock was vacation rental homes which meant that there were few people to help dig out. Most of the neighbors on the Outer Banks changed weekly. In the winter months, you could go for long stretches at a time without seeing any neighbors at all.

Todd parked the truck in the Sunoco parking lot. The gas station was still closed. After all, you can't pump gas without electricity. Even though Riss and Lou were insistent on splitting up, Todd worried about their safety. "We really don't know what we'll run across on each of these streets. Better that you two stick together."

Despite her best protests, Riss agreed that she and Lou would search together. Since they had no means of communicating, Todd brought along two whistles.

"We should each be on parallel streets at all times, which means we should still be within earshot of each other in case you find something or get into trouble. Just blow the whistle three times if you find something, and once real long if you're in trouble. If you keep blowing, I'll come running to find you, and I'll do the same. All of these streets connect via a service road that runs along the sound. At the end of each street, let's wait for each other before moving onto the next. It will be slow this way, but we won't lose contact with each other."

Lou and Riss agreed, and the two search parties headed west down their individual streets towards the sound. Each group ran across folks who were out working on their yards and houses. They each asked if anyone had seen a yellow lab just before the storm.

"No, he didn't have a tag or a collar," Lou, Riss, and Todd would each explain. There was such sadness and pity in the voices of the folks from the neighborhood when they said they hadn't seen anything.

Going down each street was a learning experience in how hurricanes work. You would think that if one house was damaged, they'd all be equally damaged, but that was not entirely the case. Based on the geography and elevation of the street itself, some houses incurred water damage from the back half of the storm, some sustained wind damage from the front half, some sustained damage from both halves, while others had no damage at all. Sure, the damage to landscaping was evident everywhere, as were the downed power lines, but what remained constant as they walked down each street was that the people they encountered appeared to remain as upbeat as they could be. No one was going to let a storm damage their spirits. Sure, the storm may have damaged property, but it hadn't damaged their attitudes.

Todd and his neighbors walked up and down the side streets until they got about a mile away from the truck. Neither group blew their whistle to get the other group to come running; there was just no sign of Jack, nor had anyone noticed him prior to the storm or immediately after. At this point upon meeting on the service road, they each decided to walk five more streets before doubling back to the truck. After five more streets, there was still nothing. So, they made their way back to the Sunoco station and decided to start taking on the streets of Old Nags Head Cove, a housing development that had been there as long as Todd had been on the Outer Banks.

They moved the truck down the street to the Cove and began searching in a similar pattern as before. Luckily, they were able to cover most of the neighborhood by truck. The roads were not as clogged by debris as the beach had been. They would stop every few feet to yell Jack's name, the only noise to disturb the hum of chainsaws and the banging of hammers. Of course, there was still no sign of Jack. Although, one person said that he had seen an animal walking south along the bypass just prior to the storm, whether it was Jack or not, he couldn't be sure.

After Old Nags Head Cove had been searched thoroughly, Todd was becoming more and more despondent, concerned that he was never going to find the dog. He did feel like he owed it to Jack to keep trying, however. After the Cove, the trio decided to try between the highways.

This is the area of side streets that runs perpendicular to both the bypass and the beach road. The same set of rules was in place: three short blows on the whistle if you find something, one long one if you were in trouble.

They would also meet at the end of each street on the beach road before moving onto the next street. They did this for about a mile with no results. It was getting late into the afternoon, and at this point, Todd decided to call off the search for the day. He had promised Zach that he would be over to help him with his damage, and he needed to get there well ahead of dark.

Todd, Riss, and Lou drove back silently to Kitty Hawk. At one point during the ride, Riss tried to pick up Todd's spirits by reminding him of how smart a dog Jack was. "You didn't raise him from a puppy; he survived on his own until you stumbled upon him. Certainly, he's been through a storm or two and managed to be ok."

Todd nodded in agreement. Jack had gotten along alone for a while and was still largely a dog that survived by instinct. Todd didn't own him, after all. He had no rules and he didn't keep him caged. For the most part, the dog did what he wanted when he wanted, and he got along just fine that way. Todd dropped the young couple off at their home in Kitty Hawk. He thanked them for giving up their day. He explained that he had to go out and help one of his crew clean up and would not get home until after dark, so he'd see them tomorrow. Todd backed the truck out of the driveway and headed for Zach's in Kill Devil Hills.

When he got there, he was happy to see the other two guys in the crew already there lending a hand. They had gotten the tree off the corner of the house and had it lying on the ground. Zach was making short work of it with his chainsaw. "Hope you don't mind boss. I had one of the guys stop by the shop and grab it for me."

"No worries. Whatever we need," Todd replied. "Did you guys also grab those blue tarps? We'll need them to cover up the hole in the roof."

"Yeah, we grabbed them too. You can take it out of my paycheck."

Todd glared at Zach. "Of course, I'm not going to take it out of your check. We're more than a place of business, we're family. Family helps family, jackass. But I'll tell you what you will do."

"Almost afraid to ask," Zach said. "What's that?"

"The next time we stop at the Happy Dolphin after work, I'll let you buy me a beer, maybe three."
Zach, relieved at the answer, replied, "But you're the one who makes the big bucks, not me. Remember, before you bought the company, you were me, so you know I can't afford your fancy beer."

Both men were laughing now. "Yeah, good point. Maybe I'm using you all wrong. Maybe instead of doing labor, I should have you out soliciting new business."

"Why's that boss?"

"Well, here I am giving up my time and using my tools to help you with your clean up, and all of a sudden, I now owe you three beers. Touché Zach. Touché."

Todd, Zach, and the other two workers labored until the sun started to set. They didn't patch the hole in the roof for a couple of reasons.

First, Zach had to file a claim with his homeowners' insurance. Second, they didn't have any building materials to do it with. Without power, the lumber yard, as was the case with every other business on the Outer Banks, hadn't been able to open their doors yet for business.

The other two crew members had to walk to Zach's from their houses. Their streets were still blocked off. So, Todd walked with them back to his truck, which was sitting on the bypass, and drove them to their streets. He thanked them for helping and hoped they could all get back to work in a couple of days.

Night had now hit the Outer Banks. It had been 48 hours since Izzy had blown through. Even though she was now dead, the destruction she left in her path would be felt for a long time.

As Todd was driving home, Ocean 105, which was still operating with generator power, reported that the Governor of the state had declared Dare County, the county named after Virginia Dare -- the first child born in the new world from English parentage and the home of the entire Outer Banks -- a disaster area. "Hopefully," Todd thought, this will help speed things up, in terms of restoring power and communications.

It was also reported that help was on the way. Power companies from Virginia, Maryland, and West Virginia were on their way to help get things back to normal. Once that's done, people can get back to work, open up their businesses, and restore a sense of normalcy to replace the chaos that they've been living under for a couple of days.

Todd got home, parked the truck under the house, and walked down to where the pier had once been on the sound. As he did, he noticed that Lou and Riss's SUV was missing from their yard.

Maybe they had gone down to the hardware store to check things out. "Good for them," he thought. It's time to stop doing nothing." Todd got to the sound and looked west in the direction of the town of Manteo on Roanoke Island. It was eerily dark. Normally, on a night like tonight, you would see it all lit up across the water, but now, it was almost like it didn't exist. There were just a couple of lights, but that was about it. Those are, no doubt, the ones with generators. He wondered if one of the lights he saw was Chuck's. He wondered if Kim was there with him and Trish. He wondered if Kim was as sick with worry about him as he was about her.

"Carrier pigeons!" He laughed. "That's the answer, dammit!" He yelled to the darkness. "Before the next storm, I'm going to get me a coop filled with carrier pigeons so I don't ever have to go through this again."

Kim also strolled out to the waterfront. Remarkably, the gazebo in Shallowbag Bay stood untouched from the storm. Like Todd, all she saw were sporadic lights on generator power as she gazed over towards the beach. She hoped the power and cell phones would come back to life soon. Waiting to find out if Todd was alright was becoming too much to bear. Plus, she knew that Todd had probably all but given Jack up for dead, and that he would be very depressed about it now.

Sadly, she walked back to Chuck's. It made sense for her to stay there instead of staying at home since they had a generator, and with it, they had a refrigerator, a stove, hot water, and lights.

Oh, and most importantly, they had a fully stocked wine rack. Thanks, in large part, to the wine of the month club gift.

Todd also walked back home to the dark and lonely home. As he got there, Lou and Riss pulled their SUV into their driveway.

"How's the store?' Todd called out.

"Oh, we were out there for about 15 minutes when we left you. Seems ok. Just waiting on power and a delivery truck of supplies so we can open back up," Lou said.

"Oh, I just assumed that's where you guys were just now."
"No," Riss replied. "We went back to do some more looking for Jack. We knew that you wanted to but were obligated to help your guy out, so we did some more searching for you."

"You what? You're kidding, right?"

"No," Lou responded. "We knew that you would have kept searching had you not had an obligation to your guy, so we continued the search for you."

"That is so amazing of you guys. You really shouldn't have. You have your own lives to worry about. You have a store that you need to get back open. People will be relying on you to get things done here on the Banks."

"Yeah," Lou said. "But again, without power and supplies, ain't much help we can provide right now."

Riss chimed in. "And we're going back out at first light to continue the search. You in old man?"

Todd stammered "Uh, Yeah. You sure? To be honest, I was thinking of calling off the search. If Jack was ok, I think he would have been home by now. Well, not home, because he really doesn't live here, but you know what I mean."

"Well, you can give up if you want, but Lou and I aren't. We'll be back out at first light. Good night Todd." And with that, the young couple from Cleveland, by way of Atlanta, climbed the stairs to their house and disappeared into the darkness. As Todd went into his house, he thought how nice it would be to have this young couple as friends for him and Kim. This was another reminder about much he really wanted this relationship with her to work out this time. "They don't even really know Kim, "he thought. Maybe they had seen her once or twice when they were out and about on the beach, but as far as he knew, they've never talked.

It had been a long time since Todd had eaten anything. There wasn't much in the refrigerator, but he did have some canned goods in the cupboard. He could really go for the Dinty Moore beef stew, but after a thorough search, he couldn't find it. He didn't remember eating it. "Wonder where it went," he thought. He did locate a can of Spaghetti-O's with meatballs. He opened that up and ate it right from the can. " Mmmmmmmmmmmm good," he chuckled.

Chapter 23.

There was a loud banging on the door that startled Todd awake. "Get your ass up old man! We got some searching to do!" It was Riss, of course.

"Yeah, she and Kim will get along just fine," he thought "Ok, give me a minute. I'm not as young as you. It takes me a minute."

"You got that right," Riss said laughing. "You got exactly 15 minutes to do what you got to do to get ready. Now get a move on. We'll meet you in the driveway."

"Let me just grab a quick shower and flip on the generator to make some coffee."

"Just get your wrinkly old ass in the shower. I'll make the coffee."

Todd grabbed a clean towel and was off to another cold shower. He had gotten used to taking these cold ones, but it sure will be nice once the power goes back on and he can take a shower that lasts longer than 45 seconds.

Todd finished his shower and grabbed a pair of semi-clean cargo shorts and a t-shirt. Lou and Riss were now both standing in his kitchen. The coffee was ready as Riss poured three steaming mugs. "Hope you don't mind us helping ourselves. Without power or a generator, coffee seems like a luxury for us right now," Riss said.

"No, not at all. I didn't even think about you two being without power.

You could have hung out in here with the generator. Sorry I didn't think of that sooner. In fact, let's put on another pot, and I'll throw some omelets together before the eggs go bad."

"That would be awesome," Riss said. "But let Lou make the eggs. He can cook! I'll make the coffee. You just sit down."

As Lou and Riss worked in the kitchen and Todd sat at the breakfast bar, Riss said "You know, for a bachelor, you keep a pretty neat house. I always assumed this place would be a mess inside."

"Why would you think that?" Todd asked.

"I don't know. Single guy alone. Don't really see a woman over here ever so you don't have a reason to keep the place clean. I mean, whenever I'm gone for more than a day, Lou has the house looking like a nuclear explosion went off. Nice to see a guy knows how to keep a house clean," she said, while looking straight at Lou.

"Yeah, thanks for that Pal," Lou said. "Now I'm going to be expected to pick up after myself." With that, all three of them laughed.

Eggs consumed, coffee drained. The three headed out to begin their search for the day. Todd not holding out as much hope as the young couple seemed to have. Today, they would head further south and cover all the area south from the where they stopped yesterday to Whalebone Junction. Todd thought while there, he would look at the progress of the causeway to see when that might be open.

On the drive down, Riss, the ever inquisitive one, asked Todd, "So why is it we never see a woman at your house? You gay or something?"

"Riss!" Lou yelled out. "Why would you ask him that?"

"Well," she replied, "There is a big gay community down here, and he does keep his house very clean. Plus, we've never see Todd with a lady."

"I'm sorry, Todd," Lou apologized. "Sometimes Riss just speaks her mind whether it's appropriate or not. It's the thing I loved about her before we got married. Now that we're married, it's the thing I hate."

Todd was laughing. "No! God no! It's all pretty complicated, really. I have been dating this woman from Manteo on and off lately, and it seems like it's been more off than on. Sometimes I feel we're like oil and water and that we don't mix. She's a real free spirit, a surfer chick. When we do click, we click really tight. I guess she has pretty much ruined me for all other women. As much as I would like to date someone else, I just can't. It feels like I'm cheating on her even though we aren't actively dating."

"Sounds to me like someone's in love," Riss exclaimed.

"Well, ironically, we both said that in a casual phone conversation just recently. I don't think either of us meant to say it. It just came out. I also came to the realization during this storm that I need to figure out a way to make this work."

"Did she make it through the storm ok?" Riss asked.

"I don't know. I haven't been able to get in touch with her since all of the cell towers are down, as is the internet," Todd answered.

"Oh, yeah right," Lou said.

"Oh my gosh. This whole time Lou and I just thought you've been worried sick about Jack, but you've also been worried about this girl on the island too?"

"Yeah, that's about the size of it. Her brother Chuck lives down the street from her. He's a good friend of mine. I'm really glad he's there. Makes me feel better about the whole situation right now."

"Well, thank God for that," Riss replied. "But why has Kim not locked you into a relationship?"

"Marissa!" Lou yelled out. "Sorry Todd, there's that point of blank frankness that she's so good at."

"No, seriously," Riss responded, "I mean, you would be a great catch. You're certainly a compassionate person. Look at the way you took control and cleaned that older couple's yard for free. In fact, you rallied the entire street to do it. You're out looking for a dog who you keep saying isn't even yours. You helped one of your guys clean up their yard. And you told each one of your employees not to worry about working right now, and that you'd somehow still get them paid. If you weren't so old Todd, I could even go for you."

"If you weren't married, also. Right Riss?" Lou asked.

"Oh, yeah. That too," she said.

All three had a good laugh, as Todd blushed. "Well, something came over me, and I decided I'm not going to let her get away this time. I just hope all is ok over on the island."

Todd, Lou, and Riss arrived at the spot where the young couple left off their search yesterday. Todd was impressed with how much ground they covered. It would be the same procedures today. Armed with their whistles, off all three of them went. Lou went with Riss, and Todd went alone. As he watched them go off hand- in- hand down the first side street, he found himself longing even more for a stable relationship with Kim. The question was — would she be mature enough for one?

They would walk down one street, meet on the service road, and then walk back up the next road, while at the same time, yelling out Jack's name. Todd recalled back to the day when Jack came straggling up his driveway. It was a couple of years ago. He looked hungry and tired, so Todd gave him some of the food that he was just finishing. That seemed to be all that it took, because after that, Jack never left Todd's side. It may have been the one act of kindness that man had ever given that animal. A few days after, Jack bunked down on the deck and didn't appear to ever be leaving. Todd got him the doggie bed and took him to the vet for a checkup. The vet believed that Jack was about two years old. Jack also seemed to have been surviving on his own for a while. Maybe someone moved and couldn't take Jack with them, so they abandoned him as a puppy; it was all speculation. So, Todd put out the cash to make sure that Jack had all the shots he needed. The vet needed to have a name to put down in his records and asked Todd for one. "Name?" Todd hadn't even thought about that. He didn't even think about the dog being his as he just kind of showed up and stayed. Todd certainly didn't spend time thinking about a name. So, he just blurted out the first name that came to him. "Jack," he said. "His name is Jack."

"Jack? Said the vet. "Hmmm, interesting. Why Jack?"

"I don't know," replied Todd. "You asked me for a name, and I panicked. It was the first one I happened to think of. I hate when people name their animals stupid, cute names like "Fluffy" or "Muffin." Jack seems like a solid name for a solid dog. Besides, my mother was a big John F Kennedy fan when I was a kid, so I always thought of naming a kid Jack."

"Well, there you have it," Todd thought, as he continued his search for the dog that wasn't really his. "This dog and I have a history together and perhaps, like my relationship with Kim, I've been reluctant to commit to it. I'm already going full into this relationship with Kim once we get past this storm BS. If I ever find Jack again, I will get him a collar, dog tags, and finally admit he's my dog." Apparently, all it took was a huge and powerful storm named Izzy to get his life into perspective.

While searching for Jack, Riss had a nagging feeling moving forward. "Suppose he's already backtracked to an area we've already checked?" She said to Lou.

"Yeah, I thought the same thing," Lou responded. "But I gotta tell you, the longer we look, the less likely I think this is going to have a good result. I would have thought that Jack either would have come home on his own by now, or another family, seeing him abandoned with no collar and no tags, had adopted him. It's not strange for animals to be displaced in a large storm like this. Plus, he may not have even made it through the hurricane. I mean, what are the odds, right?"

Riss, ever the positive one in their relationship, had to now agree. "Yeah, I probably would have given up by now, but there's just this inner sadness in Todd that makes me want to press on. Let's give it the rest of today, and then we'll probably have to face the facts. I really don't think Todd would have been out today looking if it weren't for us."

The trio met on the service road again. They decided to try the area between the highways as they continued to move their way north. If there was any positive to the day, they noticed power crews all throughout the beach while they were out looking. With any luck, power would be restored before the day was over. That would be a godsend to the Outer Banks. Lou and Riss could open their store and provide whatever supplies they had left as people continued the storm clean up.

"Good," Todd thought. "What this place needs right now is some normalcy. People need a place to go each day to communicate with one another. Right now, everyone's lives are upside down as they spend their third day without any communication with the outside world." With that, the Coast Guard Jayhawk flew overhead, heading south to assess more storm damage on Hatteras Island.

Todd and the kids searched the better part of the day. It was about 3:00, or so they thought, when they decided to call it off. Funny, without cell phones, time just seemed to be a non-entity. No one wears a watch anymore. There's no need when you have a phone in your pocket with the time built into it. But without any cell service, there was no way to keep track of time. Besides, at this point, their cell batteries were long dead. As they headed their way back north, they noticed that pockets of neighborhoods now had power. "If they were lucky, Kitty Hawk might also be one of them," they thought. Todd told the kids that it was pointless to keep up the search. He may have to just admit at this point that he will likely never see Jack again. "No point to keep wasting any more time searching." Riss and Lou reluctantly agreed.

"Such a shame," Riss said. "Before the storm, we really didn't know you or Jack.

After the storm, we feel like we know Jack but will never see him again." And with that, she began to cry.

As Todd drove further north, the traffic lights at both Colington and at Kitty Hawk Roads were now working. That was a good sign. That meant power was at least close. As they turned left off the bypass and onto their street, they also noticed that the lesbian and the older couples both had power. "Looks like we have electricity folks," Todd suggested that while they were out, they should run down the street to check the hardware store. "Let's see if you folks are back in business again."

They ran down the street to the store. Lou pulled the keys out of his pocket to activate the automatic steel door that served as the hurricane shutter, and the trio went inside. It was pitch black since all of the windows had been covered to protect them against the storm. Lou felt with his hands all the way to the back of the store, where the circuit breaker box was located. He flipped each one to the "On" position, and one by one, the overhead fluorescent lights came to life, blinking at first but then staying illuminated. "Looks like you kids are back in business. Now who do I speak to about opening a commercial account?"

"That would be Riss," Lou said. I hope you have outstanding references because she's tough!"

They all laughed as they left the building, and Lou locked up behind them. "Well Riss," he said. "Looks like we best set the alarm in the morning. It's likely to be a long day."

Always the business minded of the two, Riss replied. "Yeah, we better come in a couple hours before opening and inventory exactly what we have."

When they got back to their houses, Todd thanked them for all the searching help that they'd provided the last two days. "Don't forget," he said, "One day soon I owe you fish tacos at the Happy Dolphin."

"No worries," Riss said. "We're not going to let you forget. Seriously, if there's anything more we can do to help with either Jack or Kim, please let us know."

"I will. Thanks."

And with that, each went into their houses.

Chapter 24.

The electricity and cable were back on which meant Todd was finally able to see the news and all the pictures that were shot from the US Coast Guard Jayhawk helicopter the past few days. What still wasn't back on was the internet and cell phones. So even if they could see out and be seen, the Outer Banks still couldn't communicate with the outside world. It was almost like that *Truman Show* movie that Jim Carrey starred in a few years back. In that movie, Jim Carrey starred as an unwanted baby raised by a corporation inside a simulated T.V. show. That's how Todd felt. People could watch him, but he can't communicate back; his life had become a reality show.

The pictures shown from overhead by the helicopter were absolutely horrifying. The devastation that was wrought on Hatteras Island was so great that the words describing it on the radio couldn't do it justice.

Homes were completely torn from their foundations. Roofs were totally ripped from their buildings. Large boats were carried by the wind and the flood waters to points greater than a mile away from their original moorings. Highway 12 was nearly washed away. A new inlet had been forged through the solid land causing even more transportation difficulties for those still stranded there. The Herbert C Bonner Bridge over Oregon Inlet had extensive damage. A ferry service was going to be needed to get people, building materials, and manpower both on and off the island.

Further north, the damage was also quite evident. The Manteo-Nags Head Causeway, the road that connects Todd to Kim, although not a total wash out like Highway 12, was still going to need extensive work done before it would be made passable again. Thankfully, that work had already been started because manpower from both sides had been able to get to it. According to the reports from the state, they were hoping that the causeway would be cleared for traffic again in the next couple of days. Unfortunately, there was no word on when cell phone or internet service would be restored.

FEMA, the Federal Emergency Management Agency, is an organization that was created back in 1978 to coordinate a response to a disaster that overwhelms both the local and state authorities, was formerly requested by the governor to provide some sort of communication to help survivors connect with family and friends who were not on the Outer Banks.

They were able to airdrop some satellite phones to local authorities on Hatteras Island, who in turn set up communication shacks at the evacuation shelters. The lines were long, but it was worth the wait to be able to tell the outside world that we were "ok." Due to a small number of phones, those on the northern Dare areas (the beach and Roanoke) had to wait. The devastation there was not as great, so the head of FEMA deemed the urgency was also not as great.

The American Red Cross was also doing what they could for those on Hatteras as well. They were airdropping food and medical supplies. The authorities were spread awfully thin ensuring that people received only what was appropriately theirs.

The pictures and sites of Hatteras were very troubling. How one storm could wreak so much havoc was almost beyond comprehension.

Todd, further watching the reports, saw the footage as the helicopter flew over Manteo. Even though he couldn't pick out Kim's house from the air, he did recognize the neighborhood. The devastation there was nothing compared to what he had just watched. Todd took a moment and said a silent prayer of thanks; one simple fly- over took about a thousand pounds of weight off of his shoulders.

He hadn't been able to talk to Kim yet or drive over to Roanoke Island, but at least it didn't seem like a life or death situation over there. In fact, the statistics were already starting to come in. A dozen people had been killed during Izzy on Hatteras Island. Another 75 were injured, and as many as 400 people were homeless. The news coverage cautioned people that these were just preliminary numbers and they could go up as the time went on.

Todd had seen enough. He flipped the T.V. off and went and sat out on his deck. The stars were as brilliant as he'd ever seen them before on the Outer Banks; there were so many and they were so bright. The moon hung over the Atlantic Ocean. The sky was so peaceful it almost made the past couple of days seem surreal. What was today anyway? Was it Thursday or Friday? He didn't even know. There was something about having a communication system--cell phones, the internet, or T.V. – to keep you informed that time was marching by each day. You wake up to a new day, and the media is ready to tell you about what happened the night before while you were sleeping. Once you're awake, they're ready to tell you about what you can expect in the upcoming day. They made sure you knew if it was Hump Day, or TGIF, or Halloween, or any other special day. Now, there was almost something nice about not having to worry about exactly what day or time it was. You just lived. You weren't living with a countdown to what was left in the day, week, month, year, or more importantly, your life.

Todd went to bed, but sleep did not come easily. The images of the storm, the numbers of people and families affected, the property damage, and his worry about both Jack and Kim were just too much, and he could not automatically turn off his brain. Usually Todd had no trouble sleeping. An honest day's work and a life of treating people right will do that for you, but not this night. Todd tossed and turned all night. He got up. He walked around. He took a shower, but nothing allowed him to relax. He turned the T.V. back on, but not to listen to the news or storm coverage. He found an old episode of Johnny Carson on Antenna TV. This particular show featured one of Todd's favorite comedians, Jimmy Brogan, in one of his first *Tonight Show* appearances. Jimmy was also a Cleveland native, and in fact, Todd and he had both gone to the same high school, although at different times. Jimmy eventually became a writer on the Tonight Show with Jay Leno for nine years. Todd watched Jimmy perform, and finally, he fell asleep. That may not sound like a glowing recommendation for a comedian, but it was the familiarity of the show that enabled Todd to feel at ease enough to relax.

Chapter 25.

Todd woke up to the sound of the waves crashing on the beach, one of his favorite sounds in the world. He didn't know exactly what time it was since his clock had been flashing 12:00 since the power came back on. He gathered his wits about him and went down to the outside shower. "Aww, hot water, finally!" He didn't have to run in and run right back out because the water felt like it had melted off a glacier. Todd stood there under the hot water for a good long while.

While in the shower, he formulated a plan. He knew his guys would still not be reporting for work because he told them to stay put until communication was established once again or until he came and got them. He knew that they would be getting cabin fever real soon. So he decided to take a ride up to the Hyatt to see if the road was clear all the way up and if they could actually get started on any clean-up work there. He finished his shower and went upstairs to make a pot of coffee. Once that was drained, he felt hungry. Todd hadn't eaten much since the night the storm hit. If he was lucky, with the power back on, he could hit Hardee's on his way up the beach and grab an egg and sausage biscuit. Hell, maybe he'd even grab two!

As Todd went out front to climb into his truck, he took a look around to see if Jack may have happened to return. Of course, he hadn't. He also noticed that Lou and Riss's SUV was missing from their yard. "Must have gone into the hardware store early this morning," he said to himself. He decided he'd also pay them a visit on his way north to the Duck - Corolla line.

Everyone decided to hit the Hardee's. There were more cars in the drive thru line than he had seen on the roads since Izzy vacationed on the Outer Banks.

He grabbed three biscuit sandwiches and three coffees and made his way to the Hardware store.

As Todd pulled in, he noticed the open sign was not yet in the window. He banged on the back door and a few minutes later, Riss swung open the big metal door, surprised to see Todd standing there.

"Well, good morning neighbor," she said to Todd.

"Good morning to you too," he replied back. "Not open for business yet?"

"Almost. Still trying to assess what we have left on the shelves to open with."

Lou came from the front of the store and upon seeing Todd kidded him and said, "I suppose now that we're friends, you feel like you can come in and get your shopping done before the crowd."

"No. Not because we're neighbors or friends. Because I brought you an egg, sausage, and cheese biscuit and a coffee from Hardee's."

"See Lou," Riss said. "He knows exactly how to bribe you."

"Yeah, doesn't take much," Lou agreed.
The three of them sat down and ate their biscuits and sipped their coffee. The young couple filled Todd in on their business thoughts: they were hoping to open the doors in the next hour or so. Before leaving, Todd grabbed some roofing nails and shingles. He noticed there were a few missing from the roof of his house this morning and wanted to get that taken care of.

"What's your plan for today?" Riss asked Todd.

"Well, I'm going to drive up to the Duck - Corolla line and make sure the road is passable. If so, I'll go to the job site that we were working on before Izzy --that's where the new Hyatt is going in — and assess the damage. I want to see if we can start working again."

"Oh, I've heard of that new hotel going up," Riss said. I heard it's supposed to be beautiful."

"Well, it was a few days ago. I have no idea what I'll find when I get there. Thankfully, my guys and I are only responsible for the interior and outside landscaping and not for the building itself."

Once Todd gathered his roofing nails and shingles, out the door he went. He threw the supplies into the bed of the truck and he drove north, parallel to the Atlantic Ocean.

The road going into Duck wasn't too bad. There was still plenty of debris that needed to be cleaned up. He knew once phone service was back up and running, his phone would be ringing non-stop from all the non-residential landlords of the vacation homes that dotted the ocean front. "Plenty to keep us busy seven days a week until Thanksgiving," he thought. He might even have to hire some temp help to get all the work taken care of. Fortunately, he knew there would be plenty of fishermen looking for work until they could make their boats seaworthy again. In the meantime, they would have to find something to support their families.

The closer to the Corolla line Todd got, the worse the damage became.

It wasn't just debris that needed to be cleaned up, but several of the micro-hotels, the houses with 12 bedrooms and 15 bathrooms, were in various stages of disrepair, and some would have to be totally demolished and rebuilt. The haphazard loss indicated that it wasn't the full force of a storm that had been through, but rather, it was the hit and miss nature of a tornado. It was likely that this area had been hit on the front edge of the storm prior to the eye wall passing overhead. Now Todd was truly wondering how the Hyatt fared. If it was also hit by a twister, there might not be any work for his crew to do until the building was taken care of. In just a few minutes, those questions would be answered.

Todd turned left down the long road that would lead back to the Hyatt complex. The hotel and grounds were secluded from the main road; they sat about a quarter of a mile back on the sound. When he pulled into the parking lot, there was only one other vehicle there. It had Virginia plates, so he figured it was the owners of the hotel who lived in Richmond. Todd went into the courtyard and found Rebecca and Tim, the owners. They recounted to Todd their story on getting down there. What was normally a three-hour drive took nearly eight. When they finally got to the bridge leading from Point Harbor to the Outer Banks, they were met by the State Highway Patrol. Since the area had been declared a state of emergency, non-residents were not allowed into the county. After explaining to the officer, and later to the officer's boss, that they were the owners of the new Hyatt, they were finally allowed in to check on their business, but they had to be willing to travel at their own risk. The state and county could not be held accountable should anything happen to them, especially since the bridge had not yet been fully inspected.

Todd, Rebecca, and Tim then looked over the property and were not unpleasantly surprised at what they found. The building made it through the storm pretty much unscathed. There were some superficial items to attend to: a busted-out window, some missing shingles, and a rain gutter or two that would have to be replaced. But all in all, it was not as bad as it could have been. As far as the landscaping, well, the overly saturated ground did not supply the resistance that some of the swaying palms needed against the brutal wind. So, a good many of them would need to be replanted. Some of them, along with the underground sprinkler system, would need to be replaced. A couple of the palms had fallen on some of the sprinkler heads and those would need to be attended to. Todd assured Rebecca and Tim that he and his crew would be back tomorrow or the next day to begin the clean-up.

"Now, if I was only able to reach the building contractor to get the other part going," Tim said. "We're glad you decided to check out the site today, otherwise we wouldn't have been able to get in touch with you either. Makes me happy that we went with your company instead of the other. When the bids were collected, the other company pressed us hard about them being the largest on the Outer Banks and you being more of a mom and pop type organization," Tim added. "But that's what eventually made us go with you. We'd prefer to deal with an owner who isn't also afraid to get his hands dirty. You coming out here today proves we made the right decision."

Todd thanked Rebecca and Tim. He told them that he was going to be passing Don's house, the general contractor, on his way home. Don was a friend of Todd's. In fact, Don built Todd's house. He'd let Don know they were down from Richmond at the project and wanted to meet with him.

They said their goodbyes. Rebecca and Tim would be staying at the hotel at this point. They had a suite built just for them so they'd have a place to stay whenever they were down at the Outer Banks. "So, whenever Don can make it, we'll be here," Tim said.

Todd headed back down south. He hadn't realized it, but after driving the last few days to his crews' houses, then to look for Jack, and now to the Duck - Corolla line, he was in dire need of gas. On the way up, he hadn't noticed if the station in Duck was open. He hoped that it was. Otherwise, he might be walking to Don's house.

Todd cruised into the Shell station and filled up. Luckily, it was open. "Gas prices were going to soar," he thought. They always seemed to at times like this. "Better to fill up now than later when most everyone else who hadn't been driving will need to. "
On his way back to Kitty Hawk to stop at Don's house, Todd took a slight detour to Southern Shores. Don's street was still without power, and the debris made it look like a bomb had gone off. Todd told Don of the day's events at the Hyatt and then made his way to the shop. He figured if they were going to start working again in a day or two, he might as well get the equipment down from the second level.

The time on Roanoke Island was spent on mundane things for Kim, Chuck, and Trish, and of course, Jack too. Chuck took the time, along with his wife and sister, and got the pool cleaned out. He had to drain it completely once the power went back on. Then all of them swept and vacuumed the pool bottom and thoroughly cleaned the filter of any leaves and sand. Since it was the end of the pool season, Chuck decided to not refill it completely.

He'd wait until the following spring to do that. The weight of the sand and debris had caused the cover to rip and the cover's frame to bend. Chuck made a note to himself to order a new cover once he was able to get back online. He did take some tarps that he had at the OBX Outfitter's Group Store, and he fastened them over the pool to keep out any more leaves and branches that might fall. It was also fastened to keep out any animals.

After the pool was finished, Chuck and the two women made their way over to Kim's house. The first thing they had to do was to get that twenty-five foot pine tree off the roof. With two women in tow, Chuck figured that the easiest and smartest thing to do would be to just grab a ladder and climb up onto the roof with a chainsaw and cut it into manageable sized chunks. He knew that way back when his father was still living here, he had purchased a ladder and kept it back behind the garage. Kim likely didn't know it even existed. Chuck went behind the garage, hoping the ladder didn't end up as a projectile during the storm, and much to his surprise, he found it was still there. He pulled it out, leaned it against the house, swung the chainsaw over his shoulder, like he was Bruce Springsteen carrying his guitar, and up the ladder he went. It took a couple of hours, but finally the tree was off the roof and there was no apparent damage to the house.

While Chuck was up on the roof, the girls cleaned up all the branches and other debris that were laying in the yard, in addition to gathering up the pieces that Chuck threw down from above. Once they were all done, Kim asked, "Big brother, can you help me take this plywood off the windows? Then you and Trish can have your house back to yourselves, and I can stay here again." Up to that point, Kim had been staying with Chuck and Trish because her house was in a perpetual state of darkness. The plywood was totally blocking out any sunlight.

"Deal," Chuck said. "Love you sis, but you've been hampering my ability to walk around in my boxers the last few days!"

"Chuck, stop it!" Trish added. "It's been so nice having a girl around the house for a change. Your brother had to behave more civilized with you there."

The three had a good laugh knowing that Trish was right, of course. "Todd left this drill thingy," Kim said to Chuck as she fetched the power tool.

All three of their thoughts drifted to Todd. They knew he was probably miserable over on the beach cut-off from all of them. He'd want to make sure that everyone was safe, but they were each sure that he would be searching for Jack and felt bad that they had no way of getting word to him that everything was ok. They also knew that, Todd being Todd, he would be spearheading whatever clean-up needed to be done in his neighborhood and ensuring that his guys were all safe and had everything they needed. He was not the kind of guy to just sit around and wallow in his sorrow.

Once the plywood boards were unscrewed from the window frames and stacked behind the garage, Chuck told the girls that dinner was on him. They decided to grab a pitcher of beer and a bucket of clams down at PW's on the Manteo docks. One pitcher led to two, which ultimately led to three. It was nice to see the town out at PW's that night. Everyone had either been barricaded in their house or out doing some sort of clean- up the last several days. It was good to see some normalcy return to the island. Kallie, who had been a server there for the last three years, said it had been busy like this all day, ever since they opened at lunch.

All three finished up their beers and clams and formulated a plan to meet up in the morning at the store. There had been no rush, up to this point, to get it open. No one was going to want to take a pleasure paddle in the sound or rent a surf board to go surfing. They were too busy getting their lives back into shape. There were no tourists to serve just yet either. They had all been sent back at the county's borders by the state police because until the bridges and the causeway were cleared, it was still too dangerous to allow anyone back onto the barrier islands. Chuck suggested they meet at 10am. He knew Kim wouldn't be up much before then, but he also wanted to drive out to the causeway to see how much longer they were going to be held prisoner on the island. He wanted to see if there was anything he could do to move things along.

Chuck and Trish walked Kim back home taking the scenic route down the length of the docks before circling back towards the town and their homes. As they walked along the docks, they looked across the water to the beach and saw lights. That was a good sign and meant, like the island, things might also be returning to normal. Once they got back to Kim's, they were met by a very hungry and over enthusiastic Jack.

"Have you fed that poor beast today at all Kim?" Chuck asked.

"I did this morning. I grabbed a can of soup out of your pantry and opened it. If he stays here much longer, he's not going to want to go back to dog food. I'll rummage around and find something here for him."

They each said their goodbyes and agreed to see each other in the morning.

While Kim, Chuck, and Trish took care of the pool and Kim's house, Todd was busy over at the shop. He wanted to get everything down off the second level and near the door. He decided that he would gather the crew in the morning and get some work done at the Hyatt. He knew they would want to get a paycheck, and he didn't want to waste time in the morning having to fetch everything down and out onto the truck. It took him a while, but he managed to get everything into place and ready to go for the next day.

As night started to fall on the Outer Banks, Todd decided to click on his cell phone to see if it was back working again. He was met with only 10% power and no service. "Worth a try," he thought. It had been a long few days, so Todd thought he'd grab a beer and a sandwich over at the Happy Dolphin. He guessed correctly that they would be back open now that the power was back on.

Todd settled into his favorite bar stool at the end of the bar, like he was Norm at Cheers. The place didn't yell out his name, like it did for Norm whenever he walked in, but this was a comfortable place for Todd. It was a comfortable place for all of the locals, Damn Yankee or not. He ordered a Red Stripe and a crab cake sandwich. He looked around. The place was busy. He wondered how long they'd be able to stay open with food supplies not coming in for the foreseeable future. He was hoping the generator had kept their coolers going, and that he wasn't going to get tainted crab.
The bartender brought out Todd's food, and Todd ordered another Red Stripe.

"They say the bridges to both the mainland and to Roanoke Island are going to open at some point tomorrow," The bartender said as he set down Todd's second beer. "They're hoping cell and internet service will be back up too."

"I sure hope so," Todd replied. "'Cause, honestly. I'm a little afraid to eat your crab cakes right now. Who knows how long they've been sitting in a very warm cooler in the back!"

The bartender, who was also one of the owners and a friend of Todd's replied. "Tell you what. If you eat that and die from food poisoning, it's on the house."

"Great," Todd answered. "Just have them put on my headstone: I'm here because of a free crab cake at the Happy Dolphin. Just think. Free advertising for all of eternity!"

"You're an ass, Todd."

"Yeah, I've been told that before. You're not the first." With that, Todd ordered one more Red Stripe. When he was done, he headed for home.

Chapter 26.

The sun rose brightly the next morning. Each passing day helped to erase the memory of the "Storm of the Century."

"But was it really?" Todd wondered. "Was it really the "Storm of the Century" this time?" Perhaps there were two different answers to that question: one by the folks on Hatteras Island, and another by those who lived further north.

Todd woke up and, by habit, turned on the Weather Channel. Right on cue Char appeared with the Tropical Update report. It seemed like another lifetime when Todd last saw her give the report. In reality, it had only been a few days.

Thankfully, Char had a whole lot of nothing to say. The segment, sponsored by the beer company, had to be three minutes long whether there was something to report or not. Today, there was nothing.

Todd went through the rest of his routine-- showering outside, making a pot of coffee, and getting ready for work. His guys didn't know that today was going to be a work day, so he waited a bit longer before leaving that morning. He decided he'd go to Zach's house first, and then ask Zach to go to the other guys' houses. If they could work, that would be fine. If not, because they weren't expecting to, well, that would be fine too. Whoever could make it would meet at the shop and then they'd continue up to the Hyatt from there. If nothing else, Todd could put in a full day and get things started.

When Todd got to Zach's, he was met with, "Hey boss, you going soft? I expected you here an hour ago."

"Well, I didn't know if you knew to expect me or not, so I got a late start," Todd replied. I've already been to the Hyatt, and Rebecca and Tim are chomping at the bit to get things cleaned up and back on track. Would you mind picking up the other two if they want to work today and meeting over at the shop?"

"No problem, Todd," Zach said. "I saw the other guys yesterday and told them they should probably expect to work today. They were happy to hear it. Too bad about the other crew in Rodanthe. Doesn't sound like we'll get that project up and running anytime soon."

"Not likely," Todd sighed. "As soon as they can make it off Roanoke Island, which will hopefully be tomorrow, they can help us get back on schedule at the Hyatt, and then we can all move down to Rodanthe. Thanks for giving the guys a heads-up. I'll see you at the shop."

About 45 minutes later, Todd supplied his crew of three to a complimentary breakfast of eggs and cheese biscuits and coffee from Hardee's. Afterwards, they threw one of the front-end loaders on a trailer and hitched it to the back of Todd's truck. It would likely come in handy for moving some of the palms that toppled in the storm. They also grabbed the usual equipment-- backpack leaf blower, rakes, and shovels-- and made their way up to the Duck - Corolla line. Don was already there without a crew. He finally made it off his street and wanted to assess the scope of work he and his gang would be facing. He told Todd that he had just gotten his power restored overnight.

Once their meeting with Don was complete, Rebecca and Tim, who were now joined by their son Jake, met Todd and his crew in the courtyard where they had already begun their day's work.

Tim, nodding towards the 18-year-old Jake, said to Todd, "Figured you might need an extra set of hands."

Todd, looking the young man up and down, who was built like a middle linebacker, said jokingly, "You sure you're up to this young man?'

Jake, knowing he had enough strength to out work any of them replied politely. "Well, Sir, I'll do my best to hang with you old men."

Todd laughed loud and long. "Okay, we'll see what you got. We can always use another strong back."

Rebecca, ever the southern hostess, promised the men that she would have lunch for them in a few hours now that the kitchen was back up and running.

The now five man crew went about their duties. Three of the guys, including Jake, went to work on replanting the toppled palms. They had to re-dig the holes and reset the trees. Digging the holes was much easier this time given the fact that the ground was as wet as it was. Todd and one other guy went about doing the general clean-up of picking up branches, raking up debris, and resetting some of the loose sod. All five worked diligently and, as promised, a few hours later out came Rebecca with a platter full of crab cake sandwiches and sweet tea.

"Hope you boys like crab cakes and that no one has a shellfish allergy. If so, I can go back and make something else."
Todd assured her that no self-respecting Outer Banker would turn down crab cakes or be allergic to them. Their forefathers, on this narrow strip of sand, had built their lives around crabbing, and many of those original families still do.

Once lunch was finished, the crew, led by Jake, went back to work. It seemed he had something to prove, though Todd just wasn't sure whether it was to himself or to his parents. He was a young man of privilege, but he didn't want to appear that way, that was Todd's reading on him.

The crew worked until about 4 pm that day. At that point, Tim came out from the hotel with a cooler of beer and ice. It was a local brew from Richmond that he had some business interest in.

"You boys worked hard," Tim said. "I figured you might like a beer before heading home for the day."

Jake looked at the cooler but was afraid to take one. "Go ahead," Tim said to his young son. "You deserve one too. But just one!"

Todd looking to get back at the boy's earlier jab said, "Yeah, Jake. Do your best to hang with us old men."

Jake laughed and took a long pull from the beer. Judging by the boy's reaction to it, it wasn't his first beer.

After enjoying a beer, Zach said he had to get back to the family, so everyone climbed back into their trucks to head for home. First, since they were going to need it again the following day, they moved the front-end loader into the maintenance shed on the hotel's property, rather than trailering it all the way back to Kitty Hawk.

While the boys were working that afternoon, unbeknownst to them, cell service had been restored.

Kim and Chuck were down at the Roanoke Island Outfitters Group store with Jack, who was running up and down the aisles having a grand old time, when they heard the announcement on Ocean 105. She and Chuck were doing their best to open their doors the following day. They knew there would likely be little or no business, but getting back to the normal day-to-day was important now. As soon as they finished up their work, Kim rushed home to grab her phone to call Todd. She was excited to find out how he made it through the storm and to let him know that both she and Jack were safe. The cell service was up, but his phone went straight to voicemail. Based on past experiences, it didn't surprise her.

The other big news of the day was that the Manteo-Nags Head Causeway was expected to be open before sundown tonight, once again allowing traffic to flow back and forth to the beach and Roanoke Island.

The store was ready to go for the re-opening tomorrow morning. Kim and Chuck worked hard throughout the day getting things ready. The kayaks were moved back outside, the shelves stocked, and debris was cleaned up in the parking lot. They went back to Chuck's house where Trish had dinner ready for the three of them, and they quickly chowed down on three steaks, baked potatoes, and corn on the cob.

"Have you contacted Todd yet Kim?" Trish asked.

"No, but not for a lack of trying," Kim replied. "But you know Todd, he never pays attention to his phone. You'd think maybe this time he would though, you know, considering the circumstances."

"He probably doesn't even know cell service is back up yet," offered Chuck. "And even if he did, it's likely his phone is dead from not having charged it over the last few days."

"They said the causeway will be open by dark. Maybe I'll just take Jack with me and we'll make a run over to the beach once it does."

Keeping Ocean 105 on in the background, they finished up dinner and waited for any word that the island and beach were now open.

Back in Kitty Hawk, Todd, figuring that he still had a little more than two hours of daylight left, got out his ladder, roofing nails, and shingles and went to work on fixing the rest of his property damage. He put on a pot of coffee as his dinner. Lou and Riss' SUV was still gone from their yard. "Probably been a busy day for the kids. Everybody needed supplies today, no doubt." Coffee in hand, Todd climbed the ladder and went to work on the roof.

Chapter 27.

With the last of the dishes in the dishwasher and the kitchen completely cleaned, word hit the airwaves of Ocean 105: the Manteo-Nags Head Causeway was now open! After several very long and arduous days, traffic was once again allowed to flow from Roanoke Island to the beach, and vice versa.

"Get going!" Trish exclaimed to Kim. "You know he's worried about you, and I'm sure he's given that poor dog up for dead by now!"

Chuck, ever the big brother, wished her a safe trip to the beach.

Kim grabbed her keys and led Jack, who sensed something big was happening. He happily leaped into the Jeep and settled into the shot-gun seat. Kim jammed the Jeep into reverse, then into first, and then put the Jeep through all six speeds of its manual transmission as she raced for Kitty Hawk. As she expected, once she got to the causeway, the road was pretty much bumper to bumper in both directions, as each side crawled to their ultimate destinations. "It felt like a prison sentence was up and now everyone was able to travel outside the prison gates," she thought.

"No worries boy," Kim cooed to Jack. "We'll have you home to see your daddy very soon. I just hope he's half as happy to see me as he will be to see you."

As she was driving, Kim was taken aback by the piles of debris that were stacked along the causeway road: trees, boats, and bits and parts of buildings from the nearby Pirates Cove housing development. It almost felt as if you were driving through a tunnel. She could now see why it took so long to open back up.

Chapter 28.

It was a beautiful Fall, picture perfect, early evening. The skies were blue. That shade of blue that the locals would often refer to as "Carolina Blue." The winds were gentle, almost as if they were asking for forgiveness as they caressed each person they came into contact with. You couldn't ask for a better day. Many would take notice of the gorgeous day, but few would be able to enjoy it the way it ought to be enjoyed.

Todd Richards, with coffee at his side, was sitting on his roof repairing and replacing shingles.

Just as the last remaining few minutes of day light shone down on him, Todd moved towards the back of the house to hammer in the last of the replacement shingles. "I should be done here just as I lose all the light of day," Todd said to himself.

As he moved to the rear of the house, he didn't hear the Jeep pull into his driveway and park next to his truck. He didn't hear the Jeep door slam as Kim and Jack got out. He didn't hear them as they scurried up the steps to the deck, nor did Kim or Jack see Todd on the roof in the rear of the house. But Jack sensed it. He started barking his fool head off. This Todd heard. At first he ignored it thinking it was a neighborhood dog. Then, the familiar barking hit him like a pile of bricks. He knew that bark. That was Jack! He was back! How was that possible?

It was then that he saw both Kim and Jack on the deck. His emotions were too much for him. Todd broke down for a second, not knowing who to hug first. Surprisingly to Kim, it was her. As they stood there in a long hug and kiss, Jack jumped on both of them making it a complete family hug.

After a long while, Todd explained to Kim that he had had an epiphany and knew that he had to make things work with them. Kim then admitted the same to Todd.

After that evening, she never went back to Roanoke Island to live.

Epilogue.

Hurricane Izzy left a lasting mark. After slamming into the Outer Banks, she took a turn back to the east and made her way up the east coast of the United States. At one point, winds reached 96 MPH on the Chesapeake-Bay Bridge Tunnel and gusts were as great as 90 MPH as far north as Ocean City, Maryland. She dropped record rainfall amounts as far west as West Virginia. Izzy ultimately maintained enough strength to stay a small Category 1 Hurricane and made a second landfall just west of Long Island, New York. Wind gusts of 85 MPH were recorded in Central Park as she caused more downed trees and power lines. The Long Island Lighting Company reported that approximately 1.4 million New Yorkers were without power, making it one of the worst power outages in the state's history. There were four deaths on Long Island: two related to heart attacks and two as a result of fallen trees. Rough waves damaged both boats and docks along the Hudson River. The storm surge destroyed 48 homes on the ocean side of Long Island. One police chief remarked that due to the hurricane, crime activity dropped because "even the criminals stayed home."

Billed as the storm that wouldn't quit, Izzy continued to move northward and wreaked havoc on New England and Canada too. Canada was completely caught off guard. As a result of the storm, the following year the country decided to establish the Canadian Hurricane Centre with weather stations on both the east and west coasts. All told, Hurricane Izzy had become one of the deadliest and costliest storms to have hit the East Coast of the United States. In her wake, she left an estimated $1.6 billion dollars' worth of property loss.

Whenever a storm is particularly deadly or damaging, its name is retired. So, the name "Izzy" was retired from the Atlantic tropical storm naming list by the Hurricane Committee of the World Meteorological Organization, based in Geneva, Switzerland. It would never again be used for an Atlantic Hurricane. The following year, Izzy was replaced with the name "Ignatius."

It was a long road back for the people of Hatteras Island; the place that Hurricane Izzy, the "Storm of the Century" wrought the most damage and heartache. In her wake, Izzy totaled 22 dead, 495 injured, and left 615 people homeless. Eventually the battered towns of Hatteras, Frisco, Buxton, Waves, Salvo, Avon and Rodanthe would rebuild themselves. They always did. That was the way of Outer Bankers. You knock them down, and they'd get back up again. Nothing was more evident of this trait than how they responded during this storm.

Highway 12 would be cleared of sand and sea water and re-built. The Herbert C Bonner Bridge, which sustained some serious mooring issues, would be repaired, although the National Park Service had to run ferry service until the bridge was cleared for traffic, which was for longer than they had ever done it before. The inlet also had to go through some significant dredging. Izzy had dumped enough sand along the channel that made it all but impassable for a boat to make its way from the sound to the sea.

The Rodanthe House sustained significant storm damage. Ultimately, moving it to its current location by the new owners probably saved it from being washed out to sea altogether. The physical building would have to be attended to before the landscape crew would be able to get in there and finish up.

Original timelines didn't matter anymore. The newly constructed decks, the ones built to match the movie decks, had been severely compromised. The decks would require a complete tear down and rebuild. The roof sustained major damage as a result of the high winds. All of the construction and landscape work would ultimately get done, however, and the house opened as The Rodanthe Inn, taking in their first guests during Memorial Day Weekend the following year. As a result of the hard work by many, the house became a crowning jewel of the area and the subject of many tourist pictures, especially by middle-aged housewives and their very bored looking husbands.

Ocean 105 FM repaired all the water damage they had sustained and received an award from the governor of the state for having "gone above and beyond the call of duty" in maintaining an on-air presence to keep everyone as up- to-date on the storm as was humanly possible. The trailer that served as the office for the general manager and the sales staff had to be replaced. After sitting in that swampy environment, it never fully dried out, so it developed mold. Ultimately, it was replaced by an even bigger double-wide trailer. The DJ's joked about having the best double-wide office of any radio station in the country.

The Roanoke Island Outfitters Group had a new managing partner. Kim opted to take that role so big brother Chuck could take some much-needed time off. He still was a fixture in the store but not from open to close, like he once had been. He now took time to vacation to places that he and Trish had always wanted to go. They hiked a good portion of the Appalachian Trail in stages. After having grown up on the shores of the Atlantic, they had always wanted to see the Pacific Ocean, so they took a driving trip up the Pacific Coast Highway also.

More importantly, Chuck was finally able to take the time to write the book he's always wanted to write -- about a hurricane that hits the Outer Banks!

The Hyatt job was completed. With the opening of the Manteo-Nags Head Causeway, Todd was able to bring both crews over to complete that job quickly. Even though they had to sit out for nearly a week, they were still able to complete it by the original scheduled date. Rebecca and Tim even wagered Todd that he couldn't pull it off. He did, and in the process, he gained a big bonus from the Richmond owners. He kept the case of beer, brewed by the company that Tim had an interest in up in Richmond, but he took the additional $5,000 and split that up amongst his guys. He was, after all, able to figure out a way to pay his guys for the lost wages. He proved, once again, that nice guys can finish first. The Hyatt opened to much fanfare a couple of months later. It turns out that Rebecca and Tim also owned a marketing company and staged the biggest campaign of a hotel opening to ever hit the Outer Banks, and it hit without warning. They called it the "marketing campaign of the century." All the local Outer Banks dignitaries, mayors, congressmen, and even fishermen from the T.V. show *Wicked Tuna* were there. Even the governor of the state was included! The hotel, one of the highest occupied hotels on the OBX, has been featured on a couple of different T.V. shows on HGTV. Todd, who was interviewed for a fluff piece by the newspaper, said he was "proud to be associated with two of the biggest tourist places on the Outer Banks in recent years," one on the north side of the Banks and the other on the south.

Jack, the dog, ended up living to the ripe old age of 18, which is almost 100 in dog years, though that was just an estimate considering no one knew exactly how old he was when he came into Todd's life.

Before passing, he was able to witness and be the "Best Dog" in Todd and Kim's wedding. He was also around for the births of their twin daughters, Georgie and Maeve, who each grew up like their mother, winning a handful of east coast surfing championships. Jack even rode out a few more storms during his life: Nor'easters, tropical storms, and even another hurricane. This time, he stayed by all of their sides, not wandering off and causing grief.

And finally, what happened with Todd and Kim? It was the classic boy meets girl story-- then boy and girl go their separate ways, and finally, an event causes them to get back together, and they stay that way and live happily ever after.

THE END.

Greg Smrdel is a stand-up comedian who has an affinity for the Outer Banks of North Carolina and her people. He's a contributor for My Outer Banks Home Magazine and performs his comedy at clubs, theaters and casinos across the country.

You can reach Greg on his website at:

www.gregsmrdel.com

Made in the USA
Columbia, SC
26 March 2018